my **revision** notes

OCR GCSE (9–1)
MEDIA STUDIES

Aaron French
Eileen Lewis
Rebecca Morris
Mike Rodgers

Series Editor:
Eileen Lewis

HODDER
EDUCATION
AN HACHETTE UK COMPANY

The Publishers would like to thank the following for permission to reproduce copyright material.

Photo credits

p.20 © 2004 UPP / TopFoto; **p.21** © Ian Hooton/Science Photo Library/Alamy Stock Photo; **p.124** both © Guardian News & Media; **p.125** © Guardian News & Media.

Acknowledgements

The authors and publisher would like to thank Maidstone Grammar School for its support and the Media students of Maidstone Grammar School for permission to use their responses to Paper 1.

Every effort has been made to trace all copyright holders, but if any have been inadvertently overlooked, the Publishers will be pleased to make the necessary arrangements at the first opportunity.

Although every effort has been made to ensure that website addresses are correct at time of going to press, Hodder Education cannot be held responsible for the content of any website mentioned in this book. It is sometimes possible to find a relocated web page by typing in the address of the homepage for a website in the URL window of your browser.

Hachette UK's policy is to use papers that are natural, renewable and recyclable products and made from wood grown in sustainable forests. The logging and manufacturing processes are expected to conform to the environmental regulations of the country of origin.

Orders: please contact Bookpoint Ltd, 130 Park Drive, Milton Park, Abingdon, Oxon OX14 4SE. Telephone: (44) 01235 827720. Fax: (44) 01235 400401. Email education@bookpoint.co.uk Lines are open from 9 a.m. to 5 p.m., Monday to Saturday, with a 24-hour message answering service. You can also order through our website: www.hoddereducation.co.uk

ISBN: 978 1 5104 2920 8

© Eileen Lewis, Rebecca Morris, Aaron French, Mike Rodgers

First published in 2018 by
Hodder Education,
An Hachette UK Company
Carmelite House
50 Victoria Embankment
London EC4Y 0DZ

www.hoddereducation.co.uk

Impression number   10 9 8 7 6 5 4 3 2 1

Year   2022 2021 2020 2019 2018

Cover photo © Jacquie Boyd from Debut Art Agency

Typeset in India by Integra Software Services Pvt. Ltd, Pondicherry, India

Printed in Spain

A catalogue record for this title is available from the British Library.

Get the most from this book

Everyone has to decide his or her own revision strategy, but it is essential to review your work, learn it and test your understanding. These Revision Notes will help you to do that in a planned way, topic by topic. Use this book as the cornerstone of your revision and don't hesitate to write in it – personalise your notes and check your progress by ticking off each section as you revise.

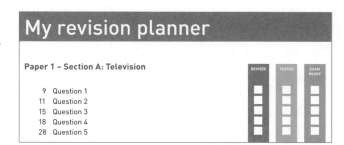

Features to help you succeed

Exam tips

Exam tips are given throughout the book to help you polish your exam technique in order to maximise your chances in the exam.

Key terms

A number of key terms are used and defined for you as you work through this guide. Make sure you learn them so that you can use the terms accurately and precisely in the exams in order to gain top marks.

How to use theory

Examiners will expect you to be able to use some theories, such as Blumler and Katz's Uses and Gratifications theory and Propp's theory of narrative. This guide shows you how and where to apply theory.

Revision activities

These activities will help you to understand each topic in an interactive way.

Exam practice, sample answers and assessment comments

Practice questions are provided for exam questions, together with some sample answers and assessment comments. Use these to consolidate your revision and practise your exam skills.

Now test yourself

These short, knowledge-based questions are the first step in testing your learning. Answers are at the back of the book.

How to prepare for the exam

These sections are summaries of how to revise for each topic.

The theoretical framework

You have learned how to analyse media products by using the following four areas of the theoretical framework:

Media language	How do the media use media language elements, generic conventions and narrative to communicate meanings to their audiences?
Media representations	How are people, places, events and issues portrayed in the media?
Media industries	How are media products funded and how are they affected by the industries that produce them?
Media audiences	How are audiences targeted and how do they respond to media products?

You will be tested on your knowledge of all of these areas in both of the examinations. This guide explains which areas are being tested in each question.

My revision planner

REVISED   TESTED   EXAM READY

Introduction

The nine media forms and the set products

In your Media Studies course, you have learned about set media products from nine media forms, all of which will be tested in the two examinations. Here is a reminder of where the nine media forms are tested and of the set media products:

Media form	Examination	Set product
Television (in-depth study)	Paper 1 Section A: Television	*Cuffs*, Series 1, Episode 1, BBC1 *The Avengers*, Series 4, Episode 1, ITV
Film	Paper 1 Section B: Promoting Media	*The Lego Movie* film
Video games	Paper 1 Section B: Promoting Media	*The Lego Movie* video game
Advertising and marketing	Paper 1 Section B: Promoting Media	*The Lego Movie* poster campaign and UK TV trailer
Magazines (in-depth study)	Paper 2 Section A: Music	*MOJO* magazine
Music video	Paper 2 Section A: Music	One pair from the following four options: 1 Wheatus – *Teenage Dirtbag* / Avril Lavigne – *Sk8er Boi* 2 Mark Ronson, Bruno Mars – *Uptown Funk* / Beyoncé – *If I Were a Boy* 3 The Vamps, Demi Lovato – *Somebody to You* / Little Mix – *Black Magic* 4 Tinie Tempah, Jess Glynne – *Not Letting Go* / Paloma Faith – *Picking Up the Pieces*
Radio	Paper 2 Section A: Music	*Live Lounge*, BBC Radio 1
Online news (in-depth study)	Paper 2 Section B: News	*Observer/Guardian* website and social media
Newspapers	Paper 2 Section B: News	Two contemporary front covers of the *Observer* and the front covers of: the *Observer*, 30 October 1966 the *Observer*, 6 November 1966 the *Observer*, 20 October 1968 One complete contemporary print edition of the *Observer*

What you have to do in the exams

The exam papers

You will have to complete two examination papers, each worth 35 per cent of your final grade:

- **Paper 1: Television and promoting media** lasts for 1 hour and 45 minutes, including 30 minutes for the screening of the extract.
- **Paper 2: Music and news** lasts for 1 hour and 15 minutes.

Paper 1 **Television and promoting media** 70 marks 9 questions	**Section A:** Television (in-depth study)	Five questions (including three questions on the unseen extract from either *Cuffs* or *The Avengers*)	45 marks
	Section B: Film marketing Video games Advertising and marketing	Four questions	25 marks
Paper 2 **Music and news** 70 marks 10 questions	**Section A:** Music videos Magazines (in-depth study) Radio	Five questions	35 marks
	Section B: Online news (in-depth study) Newspapers	Five questions	35 marks

Creating media

The remaining 30 per cent of your grade will come from your major practical production. It is possible that you will have completed your production before you start using this guide, but in order to maximise your marks for this non-examined component we have included some checklists at the back of this book.

The checklists highlight the importance of reviewing the detailed requirements of the brief you have chosen and help you to ensure that you have covered all the necessary areas in your Statement of Intent, which must be submitted with your production.

Paying attention to these details will help you feel confident that you have done your best in this non-examined component before you tackle your exams.

Contexts

Knowledge and understanding of the influence of media contexts will be tested in Paper 1 Question 5 and in Paper 2 Question 10.

In addition, one analysis question across the two exam papers will ask you to refer to media contexts in your answer. This question could be asked in Paper 1 Questions 2, 3 or 9, or in Paper 2 Questions 4, 5, 8 or 9.

In order to answer these questions, you will need to apply social/cultural/political/historical contexts such as:

- **changes in gender roles**
- **changing attitudes to sexualities**
- **multiculturalism**
- **celebrity culture**
- **consumerism.**

You will find detailed explanations of contexts, together with activities and examples to help you apply contexts to questions, throughout this guide.

> **Changes in gender roles**: the increasing role of women in public life (e.g. politics) following the impact of 1970s feminism.
>
> **Changing attitudes to sexualities**: the increasingly visible role of LGBT people in public life, and acceptance of different sexualities.
>
> **Multiculturalism**: the change from a white society in which racism is 'normal' to one characterised by many different racial and ethnic groups.
>
> **Celebrity culture**: the organisation of popular culture around celebrities – people who are famous for being famous.
>
> **Consumerism**: the expectation that people will aspire to 'better themselves' by buying goods and services (e.g. clothes, cars, houses) that mark out their individual identity. (Opposing ideas to consumerism may include: to reject material goods or to follow one's duty to a group or society.)

▶ Paper 1 – Section A: Television

What you have to do

Section A of the exam asks five questions on your in-depth study of television and covers the whole of the theoretical framework.

You will have around 30 minutes of screening and note-making time and then around 45 minutes to answer Section A. As this section is worth 45 marks, this means that the exam equates to roughly 1 mark per minute of writing time.

Which areas of the theoretical framework must I study?	
Television	The whole theoretical framework: ● media language ● representation ● media industries ● media audiences plus social, cultural and historical contexts.

Television

Television is one of the bigger 'in-depth' studies that covers the whole theoretical framework and the first three questions will be based on a three-minute unknown extract.

The five questions will be as follows:

Q1	5 marks	This will be an analysis question on the extract and is likely to be on media language, taking around five minutes to answer.
Q2	10 marks	This will be an analysis question and may be based on media language and representation or other areas of the theoretical framework. It will ask you to come to a judgement and conclusion. Your answer should be a short essay, taking about ten minutes to answer. The question may ask you to refer to contexts.
Q3	15 marks	This question will ask you to analyse the extract in terms of media language and representation, and come to a judgement and conclusion about it. This longer essay should take about 15 minutes to answer. The question may ask you to refer to contexts.
Q4	5 marks	This question is likely to focus on television industries or audiences, taking about five minutes to answer.
Q5	10 marks	This question will ask for knowledge and understanding of the influence of contexts on television programmes and ask you to refer to the set products *Cuffs* and *The Avengers*. This short essay should take around ten minutes to answer.

Let's start by focusing on the questions that reference the unknown extract.

Question 1 is based on the extract alone; Questions 2 and 3 may require you to refer to other elements of your full course, including different areas of the theoretical framework and media contexts. Questions 1, 2 and 3 all require you to demonstrate skills of analysis.

Question 1
What this question involves

REVISED

Question 1 is worth 5 marks and focuses on media language. It will test your ability to analyse how sound, camerawork, editing or mise-en-scène create meaning in the unknown extract. This extract will always be taken from one of the two set products, which are *Cuffs* (Series 1, Episode 1, 'Luck of the Draw') and *The Avengers* (Series 4, Episode 1, 'The Town of No Return'). The extract will be a 3–4-minute sequence from one of the two episodes. So, although we are going to explore *Cuffs* in this revision guide, you must be prepared to analyse a sequence from *The Avengers* set product, too.

Exam practice

Question 1
Analyse how sound is used in the extract to create meaning. Refer to at least two examples from the extract in your answer. [5]

Timing

REVISED

You will have around five minutes to answer this question.

What the examiner is looking for

REVISED

The examiner is looking for at least two examples from the extract of the specified media language element.

Media language questions

REVISED

Media language questions are likely to focus on one media language element (sound, camerawork, editing or mise-en-scène) and ask for at least two examples. You will need to:
- pinpoint where each specific example comes from in the extract, giving precise details
- analyse and explain how each example creates meaning or effects
- use the appropriate media terminology for the media language element.

Exam tip
Remember, the extract could come from either *Cuffs* (Series 1, Episode 1, 'Luck of the Draw') or *The Avengers* (Series 4, Episode 1, 'The Town of No Return').

Revision activity

Watch the section from the episode of *Cuffs* that begins at 00:27:53 (after the line 'I've been bled on, spat on and felt up') and ends at 00:30:56 as two of the male police officers are chasing the gang driving a silver pick-up truck. Pause the DVD as the police officer driving says the line '60 miles per hour and climbing'. This opens with four police officers sitting in the canteen in the police station discussing their day. It then **cross-cuts** to a female police officer walking with a female PCSO through a shopping precinct. Suddenly, a large JCB is driven into the window of a shop in the precinct and three robbers steal a cash machine. The female police officer radios through the registration of the truck and a chase ensues.

Once you've watched this sequence for the first time, stop and think about how it made you feel. Were you:
● worried for the female police officer during the robbery
● excited during the car chase as the police officers responded?

Remember to focus on the use of sound in this clip. Consider briefly how the different sections of the clip feel:
● How is sound used to help create the calm and relaxed feel in the canteen?
● The sequence in the shopping precinct is tense and the car chase exciting – how is sound used to create these feelings?

Now watch the clip for a second time and this time make notes about the kinds of sounds that you hear and when – use your glossary to help you with this. The third and fourth screenings of the extract are a time for you to consider the connotative effects of the sounds you have identified. Remember that you are going to be asked to refer to at least two examples from the extract, so make sure you have enough detail from the extract to include examples in your response.

Cross-cut: cutting from one action in one location to another action in another location.

Exam practice

Question 1

Analyse how sound is used in the extract to create meaning. Refer to at least two examples from the extract in your answer.

[5]

Read the sample answer and the assessment comments that follow.

Example 1

At the start of the extract there is well-known diegetic music playing in the canteen where the police officers are eating. This helps place the police officers in the real world and shows them acting as everyday people. This helps us see that the officers are similar to us and therefore helps create a bond between the audience and the characters.

The student identifies the correct use of the term 'diegetic music' and links it to a moment in the extract. They clearly analyse the effect that the use of diegetic sound has.

Example 1 (cont.)

Another way in which sound is used is when Lino, Donna, Jake and Ryan are leaving the café in pursuit of the robbers. Ryan shouts very loudly at Jake, who is staring longingly at his sandwich, which he had been waiting for, for a very long time. The amplification in Ryan's voice indicates the seriousness of the situation and Ryan's level of dedication, as well as being used as a scare factor to hurry Jake up.

The student identifies an example of the dialogue being amplified and then analyses the effect that this has. This response is worthy of a mark in Level 3.

Consider what other examples you could have included.

Exam tip

Your ability to take effective and relevant notes from the extract under timed conditions is key to your success in Questions 1 to 3. Practising different methods of note-taking whilst watching an extract from a television crime drama will help. Choose bullet points or a mind map to divide up your page into note sections for each question and use the timer on your phone.

Exam tip

Learn and understand the terms **connotation**, **denotation** and **semiotics**. Try to use them in your response to Question 1.

Revision activity

Using the same extract from *Cuffs*, analyse how camerawork, editing and mise-en-scène create meaning in the extract. Use a different note-making method for each of the remaining elements of media language.

Connotation: additional meanings and associations that can be interpreted from the detailed analysis of media products.

Denotation: a description of what we see or hear in a media product.

Semiotics: signs and symbols in Media Studies and their meanings.

Revision activity

Choose a three- to four-minute extract from the episode of *The Avengers*. Follow the steps above and consider how sound creates meaning.

Now test yourself

TESTED ☐

1 What is the mise-en-scène term used to describe lighting that creates dark shadows and extremes of light and shade?
2 What is the name of the camera angle that looks down on a subject?
3 What is the name of the edit that is used to cut from one action in one location to another action in another location?

Answers on p. 132

Question 2

What this question involves

REVISED ☐

Question 2 is worth 10 marks and may require you to refer to one or both of these areas of the theoretical framework:

● representation
● media language.

Timing

REVISED

You will have around ten minutes to answer this question.

What the examiner is looking for

REVISED

The examiner is going to be looking for you to analyse the extract in more depth than in Question 1. Depending on the wording of the question (and it's vital that you read the question carefully), you may be asked to analyse a particular part of the extract, a particular aspect of a representation found within the extract, or how the extract creates a particular feeling or mood. The examiner will be looking for accurate analysis of the extract through reference to media language elements. Unlike Question 1, where you are told which media language element to write about, here you can focus on any area(s) of media language you choose, so you are free to choose elements that suit the question the best.

A top-level response would be expected to:
- identify **at least** two examples from the extract
- show clear analysis of the extract in relation to the theoretical framework.

Exam practice

Question 2

Analyse how far the extract from *Cuffs* depicts the police's point of view rather than the criminals' point of view. In your answer you should:
- analyse aspects of the extract using examples to support your analysis
- judge how far these aspects depict the police's point of view. [10]

'How far?' questions

REVISED

There is more than one element to this question that you will need to remember: it's a 'How far?' question and so you will need to remember to make a judgement about this in your answer. You are also being asked to use examples to support your analysis, therefore you will need to identify at least two – and more likely three – clear and relevant examples from the extract in support of your judgement.

Let's start by asking some questions about the extract as a whole:
- Who do the viewers spend the most time with?
- Who does the director want us to feel sympathy for and care about?

Once we've considered this we should then begin to identify how the extract establishes these things.

The extract places the viewer with the police for the majority of the time:
- We spend time with Ryan, Lino, Donna and Jake in the canteen, and each officer is shown in **close-up** or **medium close-up** during this part of the extract, allowing the viewer to see their faces clearly.
- The extract cross-cuts to the shopping precinct and the viewers are immediately placed with the PCSO and female police officer as they chat. The camera **tracks** backwards, listening in to their conversation.
- Later in the sequence the viewer is placed inside the police car with Ryan and Jake as they pursue the criminals – the criminals are seen from the perspective of the chasing police car.
- The **narrative** of the sequence follows the police goings-on. When the viewers see the criminals arrive, it is into the world of the police.

> **Close-up**: head and shoulders of a subject in the frame.
>
> **Medium close-up**: head, shoulders and chest of a subject in a frame.
>
> **Tracking**: camera moves towards, away from, or sideways alongside the subject.
>
> **Narrative**: the way in which the story (factual or fictional) is told to the audience.

- The costumes of the criminals appear quite stereotypical and do not reveal their individuality.
- Sinister **non-diegetic** music begins only once the criminals arrive.

As a result of this analysis, you could argue that the extract is set up to favour the police perspective rather than that of the criminal. But of course, you could disagree – as long as you provide an analysis and refer to examples from the extract.

Let's look at how Student 1 answered the previous Exam Practice question.

> **Non-diegetic**: sound from outside the fictional world.

Example 1

The majority of the camera shots are of the police officers, who are represented as heroes, rather than villains. This is because Cuffs is favouring and supporting the police over the villains to make the audience aware that the police are very important and they should respect them.

The first few camera shots are of the four officers eating at a café. The camera position is at the head of the table so you can see every officer in the shot. This makes the audience feel very involved with the police as if they were seated at the table with them. This also engages the audience with the police even further.

After about one minute into the extract you have an idea of how the officers act and what they are like. Because the villains are only on the screen for around 30 seconds the audience does not engage and interact with them, not like they do with the police. So this is why the majority of the shots are of the police because the producers want you to interact better with the police.

The response successfully establishes that the extract depicts the police's point of view rather than the villains' in the first paragraph. The weakness in this response lies in failing to identify examples from the extract to support this. While the candidate refers to 'camera shots' twice, no specific camera shots are mentioned, such as long shot or use of close-up, and so this cannot gain Level 3. Paragraph two discusses the number of shots but not the shot type, and so the discussion of this is unfocused. Paragraph three attempts to move into editing but not in any detail; there is a vague comment about the pace of the edit but this is not clearly established. With the analysis of media language, the response would dip into the bottom of Level 2 but it lacks the detail needed for Level 3.

Example 2

In this extract we sympathise with the officers as they have much more **screen time** than the robbers. This means that we will back them and feel they may be more heroic. We see Misha instantly tell people to stay away from the crime scene, showing she cares for the civilians. Because the robbers have less screen time we see them far more negatively as we can't relate to them or know them, making them seem more villainous.

> **Screen time**: time spent in shot by a particular character or actor.

The extract also focuses heavily on depicting police officer life in a human way, so that when depicting the criminals, we are unable to bond with them as they are seen as the enemy. The criminals in the extract are seen with masks covering their faces, which hide them to us, giving a sense of mystery. Hiding their faces not only makes them less human but tells us that criminals could be anyone as the extract never gives them an identity. This creates uncertainty, which could make people feel uneasy around them.

The extract uses a variety of other techniques to see from the police's point of view and in some cases puts us in a position as if we were with them. This is seen when Jake and Ryan get into the police car and the camera is behind them in the back set at head height. This suggests that we ourselves are sitting in the car with the police officers and, together with the non-diegetic music being as fast heartbeat pace, this helps the audience experience the intensity of being a police officer.

Finally, the police officers (and criminals at some point) are shown to have great skill and teamwork. We see this with the police officers as a **bird's eye view** of the motorway follows the police car and moves directly to where the criminals are without hesitation, taking the wrong turn or being stopped. This shows how skilled they are at their job and how quickly they act on the spot, again reinforcing this idea that the extract should be viewed from the police's point of view rather than the criminals'.

> **Bird's eye view**: often called an 'aerial shot', from above the subject.

The candidate establishes early on in their answer that the extract depicts the police's point of view. The candidate also clearly identifies an example from the extract and analyses how it demonstrates this point. This second paragraph offers a further strong example to reinforce the judgement made that the extract depicts the police's point of view rather than the criminals'. In the third paragraph, the candidate refers to wider elements of media language, and provides some interesting analysis. A final point is made in the last paragraph, with reference to camerawork, and a judgement is given. This a strong Level 3 response.

Exam tip

Remember to read Questions 1, 2 and 3 carefully before you start making your notes so that you are taking notes on the right things.

Revision activity

Try analysing how the extract depicts the viewpoint of the criminals. What evidence, in the form of examples, can you find in the extract to argue the other way round?

Now test yourself

TESTED

1 What is the name of the camera movement that pivots from left to right?
2 What is a stereotype?
3 What is the name of the edit that is used to follow a conversation between two characters within the same scene?

Answers on p. 132

Question 3

What this question involves

REVISED

Question 3 is worth 15 marks. Unlike Question 1, which is based on the unseen extract alone, you will need to bring in relevant elements from your full course of study, including the following areas of the theoretical framework:

- representation
- media language
- media industries
- media audiences

and media contexts:

- social
- cultural.

Timing

REVISED

You will have around 15 minutes to answer this question.

What the examiner is looking for

REVISED

The examiner will be looking for a few things in your answer to Question 3. You are expected to demonstrate how you can analyse the extract in detail, and how you can make judgements and draw conclusions. The question will refer to the extract but you will be reminded to refer to relevant areas of the theoretical framework and contexts. There will also be some bullet points to help guide your answer. So, your answer must contain some references to the extract in the form of examples of media language and possible representations found within the extract.

As with Question 2, you can refer to any elements of media language, but remember that this question is worth 15 marks, and so you should refer to more than one area in order to reach the top levels. Along with this, you will need to bring in relevant elements from industries and audiences that you have studied. This is what the question means when it says 'refer to your full course of study'.

A top-level response would be expected to:

- analyse at least two or more detailed examples
- refer to other areas of the theoretical framework
- make judgements and draw conclusions.

Let's take a look at a sample Question 3.

Exam practice

Question 3*

In this question you will be rewarded for drawing together elements from your full course of study, including different areas of the theoretical framework and media contexts.

How far does the extract try to create a sense that it is portraying 'real life'?

In your answer you should:
- analyse aspects of the extract, giving detailed examples
- judge how far these aspects create a sense of watching 'real life'.

The asterisk (*) is there to signpost that this is an extended response answer (see p. 86 for more details on extended response answers).

Media areas and contexts

REVISED

As with Question 2, Question 3 is a 'How far?' question, so you must remember to make a judgement about this in your response.
- How does the extract use mise-en-scène to make us believe that we are watching real police officers?

The mise-en-scène is one of the most obvious areas of media language to communicate a sense of 'real life' to the audience. We see:
- police officers in costumes that we recognise to be police uniforms
- naturalistic locations (shopping precinct) and **natural lighting**
- police officers in pursuit of criminals who have committed a crime.

Which other elements of media language could you consider?
- Editing – use of **shot/reverse shot** and **continuity editing** suggests 'real life' and does not draw attention to its 'artificiality'.
- **Handheld camera** gives the extract a documentary feel, as if it's recording real life, draws us into the action and helps us to suspend our disbelief.

How could you reference your wider course of study and other elements of the theoretical framework?
- The use of recognisable **stereotypes**, such as the male criminal, helps to make the extract appear more real as this is a stereotype that is played out in other areas of the media and exists to an extent in real life.
- The use of a strong female police officer could challenge the sense of real depending on an audience's interpretation.

Thinking about further elements from your wider course, how could you bring in media audiences? Consider how audiences may interpret the extract in different ways depending on their needs.
- The extract could appear more real to those who identify with the camaraderie of the police officers together sharing lunch and who could imagine themselves involved in similar conversations.
- Those who enjoy the visual spectacle of the car chase may find enjoyment in the diversion that this offers them from real life.

Media industries, and in particular the **scheduling** choices that have been made and how they could affect the content of the programme, could also be analysed in an answer to this question.

Finally, think about how you could also bring in references to social or cultural contexts that may be explored in the extract and whether these issues help to reinforce the sense of real. For example:

Natural lighting: lighting that highlights features of the scene and appears like real life.

Shot/reverse shot: over-the-shoulder shot of one character cutting to an over-the-shoulder shot of the other character.

Continuity editing: editing that is invisible, maintaining clear and continuous narrative action.

Handheld camera: often creates juddering, urgent camerawork, like a documentary.

Stereotype: oversimplified portrayal of a member of a social group, place, event or issue, which is based on assumptions.

Scheduling: channel, day and time placement of a programme on television.

- the use of strong female police officers, a gay police officer and police officers from different ethnic groups taking lead roles within the team demonstrates equality and diversity in the modern-day workplace and is therefore reinforcing the sense of 'real life' of policing in modern-day Britain
- how this modern-day representation of policing could undermine a sense of realism depending on the audience's interpretation, their age, their experiences, etc.

Let's see how some students responded to the question.

Example 1

The extract tries to create a sense that it is portraying real life. It does this by showing us police officers doing their regular duties – we see them driving in police cars, chasing criminals and eating lunch together in the canteen at the police station. These are all conventions of police dramas.

The criminals also look like criminals and are doing criminal activities, which is what we would expect in real life. The location looks real too and it's somewhere that we would go in our real life and is often somewhere that police dramas are set.

The extract tries quite well to achieve this sense of real life.

This response begins by establishing that real life is created in the extract. It tries to underpin this with evidence by describing part of the narrative. However, it does not identify any examples of media language, although there is an attempt to discuss elements of mise-en-scène but without using any specific terms. There is little analysis, instead just a series of statements about what we see in the extract. This restricts the response to Level 1 because it lacks the examples to lift it into Level 2. The need to refer to the full course of study for this question has also been overlooked; there are no references to industries, audiences or contexts. This is required to gain Level 3. Finally, this response is brief given that the question is worth 15 marks, which equates to roughly 15 minutes of writing time.

Exam tip

Remember that for Question 3 you must refer to elements from your full course of study, including different areas of the theoretical framework and media contexts, in order to reach Level 3.

Revision activity

Try identifying evidence from the sequence that *Cuffs* either fully demonstrates real life being established or provides evidence of it not being established at all.

Now time yourself to see if you can produce a better answer in 15 minutes.

Example 2

The extract attempts to place the police officers in 'real life' with everyday people in order to make them appear normal and a part of society. This is seen in the locations used. The police officers are seen in a café, in a town centre and on the motorway. All of these locations are seen in everyday life and people go to them or visit them. Seeing the police here and not away from the public makes them appear included and part of everyday life and society.

During the chase sequence, a bird's eye view tracking shot displays the many cars, roads and roundabouts in the area of the chase sequence. This is effective at making us feel as if we are watching 'real life' as all the locations are recognisable as real, helping us to draw connections, as we would in real life, with where we may have been and what we may have seen.

However, the extract is unable to fully show 'real life' as it is unable to break certain rules of television. Many things are affected by these rules. For example, due to being broadcast pre-watershed, swearing or adult references are removed and cannot be shown as younger audiences are not supposed to be exposed to swearing or adult references.

The candidate begins by making a judgement about the role of the police in society (context) and so sets up the line of argument that the extract does establish 'real life'. The candidate moves on to discuss how mise-en-scène is used to present a series of recognisable locations, which helps to establish a sense of 'reality'. In paragraph three, the candidate analyses how the camerawork and mise-en-scène, two elements of media language, are used together to establish a setting and storyline that is believable and appears 'real'. Finally, this response succeeds in drawing together elements from the full course of study by referring to scheduling choices made by the BBC (media industries – theoretical framework) and by considering how the extract may fail to fully portray 'real life' through these scheduling decisions. This candidate provides four examples from the extract within their analyses, references the wider theoretical framework (industries) and their full-course of study. However, they do not make reference to media contexts and only imply references to representation. The response tips into the bottom of Level 3 as a result.

Revision activity

Identify at least one example from each element of media language, one example of representation, one of audience and one related to industries for this question, to test your understanding of the theoretical framework.

Exam tip

Remember that for Question 3 you must refer to elements from your full course of study, including different areas of the theoretical framework and media contexts, in order to reach Level 3.

Now test yourself

TESTED

1 Identify at least two elements of the Uses and Gratifications theory.
2 What is the word used to describe the placement of a television programme on a particular channel, at a particular time and day of the week?
3 On what channel, day and time was *Cuffs* placed?

Answers on p. 132

How to prepare for the exam

- Test out different methods of taking notes under timed conditions. Choose the one that suits your learning style best.
- Practise taking notes under timed conditions.
- Learn the definitions of the elements of media language (editing, mise-en-scène, camerawork and sound).
- Practise identifying elements of media language in other extracts from *Cuffs* and *The Avengers*.

Question 4

What this question involves

REVISED

Question 4 is worth 5 marks and will test your knowledge and understanding of television as a media form. It is likely to focus on media industries and audiences. The question may also ask you to refer to *Cuffs* and/or *The Avengers*.

Timing

Spend around four to five minutes on this question.

> **Exam tip**
>
> Make sure you do not spend more than five minutes on this question as you cannot gain more than 5 marks, however good your answer may be.

What the examiner is looking for

Examiners are looking for answers that show knowledge and understanding of media industries or audiences in relation to television. The question may focus on any one of the following:

- the requirements of **Public Service Broadcasting** (PSB)
- the **regulation** of television channels by Ofcom
- the different ways in which television channels are **funded**
- audiences' relationship with television in the UK.

> **Exam tip**
>
> You will need a number of facts at your fingertips in order to answer this question. Make sure you look at the question carefully and use the appropriate facts.

For this question you will revise:

- the role of Ofcom and the ways in which it controls broadcasting in the UK
- Public Service Broadcasting with particular reference to BBC television
- BBC funding, including debates over the licence fee
- **commercial television** funding and PSB **remits**
- the different ways in which audiences access and consume television
- how audiences are targeted by television producers
- **scheduling** and changes in technology
- Uses and Gratifications theory (Blumler and Katz).

> **Public Service Broadcasting**: broadcasting for public benefit, rather than to make money; broadcasting that is independent of government.
>
> **Regulation**: control of an institution by an authority that checks to see that it is following the rules.
>
> **Funding**: how the channel gets its money to finance programmes.

> **Commercial television**: television owned by private companies and usually funded by advertising.
>
> **Remit**: the particular responsibilities of a television channel towards its audience, as defined by Ofcom.
>
> **Scheduling**: planning the times when programmes will be broadcast in order to attract the largest or most appropriate audience. (For more information, see www.bbc.co.uk/education/guides/zc8tv4j/revision/3)

What does Ofcom do?

Ofcom regulates television and radio broadcasting in the UK, setting standards for television and radio programmes that broadcasters have to follow. Ofcom can fine broadcasters if their programmes breach (do not follow) Ofcom's Broadcasting Code.

Ofcom carries out regular reviews to see that the BBC, ITV, Channel 4, Channel 5 and S4C are fulfilling their particular PSB requirements.

Public Service Broadcasting and the BBC

The BBC has been a PSB channel since it was set up in 1922. Lord Reith (see Figure 4.1) outlined the PSB principles in 1925, stating that broadcasting should 'inform, educate and entertain', and that it should be free from commercial and government pressures. The definition of Public Service Broadcasting has developed since then, but Lord Reith's key points are still at the centre of the BBC's **ethos** today. These points are clearly stated in the BBC's mission statement, which you will find on its website: Inside the BBC: www.bbc.co.uk/aboutthebbc/insidethebbc/whoweare

> **Revision activity**
>
> Look up the BBC website 'Inside the BBC': www.bbc.co.uk/aboutthebbc/insidethebbc/whoweare
>
> Write down key points for each of the following areas, making sure that you can remember them for the exam:
> - BBC's mission, vision and **values**
> - public purposes (BBC Charter)
> - the licence fee
> - history of the BBC.

Figure 4.1 Lord Reith

The BBC's key PSB purposes

All the BBC channels must fulfil the requirements of PSB, with BBC One and BBC Two regarded as the main PSB channels. See if you can spot some of the **Reithian** principles in the list of BBC purposes below:
- to offer creative, high-quality, **distinctive** programmes (the BBC has been criticised frequently for being too similar to other broadcast channels)
- to reflect the United Kingdom, its culture and values, to the world
- to reflect, represent and serve the **diverse** communities of all of the United Kingdom's nations and regions
- to support learning
- to provide impartial news and information.

How is the BBC regulated?

Ofcom is the external regulator of the BBC, while internally the BBC is controlled by a board of 12–14 members, mostly selected by the BBC itself. The BBC is granted a licence to broadcast by **Royal Charter**, which must be renewed every 11 years (the next renewal date is 2027). The Charter sets out the BBC's public purposes (see above).

BBC funding – the licence fee

The BBC is funded by the annual licence fee (£147 in 2017). This pays for BBC television, radio and online content, and for developing new programmes. If you watch or listen to BBC programmes live on any **media platform**, including tablets and smartphones, it is a criminal offence not to pay the licence fee. This also applies to the growing numbers of people who watch the BBC's iPlayer catch-up service.

Ethos: a set of ideas, attitudes and values associated with a particular institution, such as the BBC.

Values: a set of ideas and beliefs held by an individual, a group or the whole of society.

Reithian: refers to Lord Reith, first Director General of the BBC, who developed the first principles of PSB, in particular that broadcasting should inform, educate and entertain.

Distinctive: in the context of PSB, means having specific characteristics that make the channel different from other channels, especially commercial channels.

Diversity: an inclusive approach that caters for all the varied cultural groups in our society.

Royal Charter: sets out the public purposes of the BBC, guarantees its independence, and outlines the duties of the executive committee and the BBC board.

Media platform: the way in which media content is delivered, such as smartphone, tablet, DVD, television, etc.

Debates over the licence fee

Critics argue that this type of funding is outdated in the multi-channel environment of the 21st century. They argue that the BBC should be funded by pay-per-view, subscriptions or advertising.

The BBC prides itself on its independence from government and from commercial pressures, and it argues that the licence fee is essential in order to maintain this independence. The government does have a certain amount of control over the BBC, however, as it sets the level of the licence fee. These debates about the licence fee make it all the more important for the BBC to offer distinctive programmes and to appeal to a wide and diverse audience.

> **Revision activity**
>
> Copy out a bigger version of the table below and write down three arguments for keeping the licence fee and three arguments against.
>
> | Arguments for the licence fee | Arguments against the licence fee |
> | --- | --- |
> | | |
> | | |
> | | |

Figure 4.2 The BBC licence fee applies to all platforms

Public Service Broadcasting and commercial channels

REVISED

ITV1, Channel 4 and Channel 5 are commercially funded channels (paid for by advertising), which also have to fulfil some of the requirements of PSB. Each PSB channel has its own specific remit. For example, Channel 4 has a remit to deliver high-quality, innovative (original), alternative programmes that challenge accepted views and values.

Channel 4 is publicly owned but commercially funded – this means that the money made from advertising on the channel does not go to shareholders but to finance new programmes.

Subscription-based channels such as those provided by Sky, Virgin or Netflix have no PSB requirements.

> **Revision activity**
>
> Copy out a bigger version of the table below and, using a listings magazine, list one programme from any of the main PSB channels – BBC One, ITV1, BBC Two, Channel 4 or Channel 5 – as an example of each of the following:
>
> | PSB characteristic | Programme | PSB channel |
> | --- | --- | --- |
> | High-quality content | | |
> | Innovative (original) and challenging content | | |
> | Stimulating knowledge and learning | | |
> | Informing the public | | |
> | Original British-made programming | | |
> | Reflecting the UK's cultural identity | | |
> | Representing diversity and alternative viewpoints | | |
> | Distinctive programming | | |

Television audiences

Mass and niche audiences

Both BBC One and ITV1 need to be popular and appeal to mass audiences. ITV1 has to do this in order to attract advertisers who provide funding to the channel. The BBC has to appeal to all UK citizens and offer a wide range of programmes in order to justify the licence fee. At the same time, it has to offer 'the most creative, highest quality and distinctive' programmes. The BBC manages these requirements through offering a wide variety of programmes on its stable of channels in order to target different audiences.

> **Mass audience**: large number of media users.
>
> **Niche audience**: media users with a special interest or of a specific demographic.

BBC One	A **mass audience** channel for all that aims to unite and inspire the nation with high-quality programmes across a range of genres
BBC Two	A niche channel that offers in-depth programmes
BBC Four	A **niche audience** channel that aims to be British television's most intellectually and culturally enriching channel
CBBC	A niche channel for 6–12 year olds
CBeebies	A niche channel for those under the age of 6
BBC Three	A niche, innovative, online-only channel aimed at 16 year olds to 30-somethings

Effects of technology

Technological changes mean that audiences view television programmes in a range of different ways, both on the television set and on other media platforms. For example, audiences can watch **time-shifted programmes** after they are first broadcast using a DVR (digital video recorder) or watch **streamed** programmes such as Netflix's *The Crown* on a computer, smart television or mobile device.

Despite these changes, the majority of audiences watch television on the television set. The PSB channels continue to be the most popular: each week 85 per cent of people in the UK with a television watch PSB channels. However, non-PSB channels are very popular with younger viewers (*Ofcom's Public Service Broadcasting Report 2017*).

> **Time-shifted programmes**: programmes that have been recorded, usually on a DVR, and are watched later than the time of the original broadcast.
>
> **Streaming**: a method of downloading a television programme or other media product digitally as a temporary file.

Targeting audiences – scheduling

Why do we still watch live television?

If technology has given us control over our viewing and we can watch programmes when and how we choose, why do audiences still watch live television? Appointment viewing – the idea of having to sit down at a particular time in order to watch a live television programme – may seem outdated. However, scheduling is still important for targeting audiences, particularly for the BBC and ITV.

Second screening

One of the reasons for watching live television is the increased use of social media: audiences can tweet or join Facebook discussions about live programmes during Channel 4's *The Great British Bake Off*, BBC One's drama series *Dr Foster* or Netflix's political thriller *House of Cards*. This activity has been termed 'second screening', i.e. screening that encourages audiences to be active, rather than passive and is a major factor in audiences' continued interest in live television.

> **Revision activity**
>
> How do audiences access television?
>
> Make a list of six ways in which audiences can access television programmes today.

Audience interactivity

Audience interactivity, where viewers are encouraged to vote for their favourites on programmes such as ITV's *I'm a Celebrity ... Get Me Out of Here* and BBC One's *Strictly Come Dancing*, also increases the number of people viewing live television. Choosing a particular contestant and voting for them on a regular basis during a television series increases the audience's commitment to the programme and their loyalty to the channel.

How to use theory

The active audience

Debates over the ways in which audiences consume media products have focused on whether audiences are passive or active.

It can be argued that television audiences in the 2010s are more active than audiences in 1965 for the following reasons:

- channel surfing between the wide number of available channels
- audiences can access television programmes on a number of different platforms
- second screening on social media
- interactivity with television programmes, such as voting for celebrities in game shows.

Audience ratings and *Cuffs*

Competitive scheduling can benefit the main channels as it generates publicity. In autumn 2017 the BBC scheduled *Strictly Come Dancing: The Results* at 7.20 pm on Sundays, while ITV scheduled *The X Factor* at exactly the same time and on the same day. *Strictly Come Dancing* regularly gains higher **audience ratings** than *The X Factor*, with 9.4 million people watching the first live episode, as opposed to *The X Factor*'s 4.8 million on the same night in September 2017. The audience ratings are measured by the Broadcasters' Audience Research Board (BARB).

> **Audience ratings**: the number of viewers who watched a live television programme, researched by BARB; consolidated audience ratings are time-shifted viewings within seven days of the original broadcast.

The watershed

REVISED

Ofcom makes and oversees the rules about the **watershed**, which begins at 9 pm and ends at 5.30 am. During these hours television broadcasters can show material that is unsuitable for children up to the age of 15; 18-rated content should not be broadcast before 10 pm. Unsuitable material includes sexual content, violence, graphic or disturbing imagery and swearing.

> **Watershed**: the time at which TV channels may start to show content that is unsuitable for children – currently 9 pm in the UK.

> **Exam tip**
>
> The sections below on *Cuffs* and *The Avengers* give you information that could also be useful for your answers to Questions 2 and 3, so revising this carefully could help you gain top marks!

Scheduling and *Cuffs*

Cuffs was scheduled in 2015 on BBC One on Wednesdays at 8 pm. This was **peak viewing time**, when 81 per cent of all television viewing was still watching live television as scheduled. The programme was expected to attract a mass, diverse audience by offering them a range of characters in the hope that they would identify with one or more of them. As the programme was broadcast pre-watershed, the producers had to take care over the way they portrayed crimes, criminals and the police, avoiding swearing or extreme violence. One of the ways they did this was to combine serious police procedural plots with humour.

> **Peak viewing time**: 6 pm to 10.30 pm is the time of day when most people are watching television and when advertising costs the most.

REVISED

Revision activity

Using your study of *Cuffs*, add three more ways to the list below in which the programme specifically targeted its audience.

Elements of comedy for the family audience
A range of multicultural characters for the audience to identify with
Authentic locations in and around Brighton
Exciting police chases

Production and *Cuffs*

REVISED

The BBC is expected to encourage competition for producing programmes partly as a response to criticism of the licence fee, so many BBC programmes are produced by independent companies. Tiger Aspect Productions, which produced *Cuffs*, is one of those, although we might question its independence as it is part of Endemol Shine, which in turn is 50 per cent owned by 21st Century Fox, the huge media conglomerate.

Why might audiences watch *Cuffs*?

REVISED

How to use theory

Uses and Gratifications and *Cuffs*

This theory assumes that audiences are active consumers of media products. Blumler and Katz identified four ways in which audiences might use media products and gain pleasure from them.

Personal identity – audiences:
- have a wide range of characters from the ensemble cast to identify with
- may see characters such as Ryan Draper or Donna Prager as role models
- may empathise with the difficult job of the police in the face of public indifference
- may enjoy seeing gay characters as key protagonists who are not defined by their sexuality
- can explore and/or reinforce their own values through those celebrated by the programme – professional teamwork, comradeship and dedication to duty.

Social interaction and integration – audiences:
- may feel that they are part of the team
- may build a personal relationship with a character, forgiving the character's weaknesses, admiring their achievements – almost as a substitute for real-life interaction

- may discuss the programme with family, friends or fellow workers
- may use Twitter or Facebook to comment on the programme – when the BBC announced that the second series had been cancelled, a petition to save *Cuffs* on Change.org gained about 12,000 supporters and the fan campaign following the cancellation of *Cuffs* trended on Twitter.

Entertainment – audiences:
- can escape into the fictional world of a police team working together
- can derive vicarious pleasure from seeing the characters in jeopardy, such as Jake looking terrified during the police chase on his first day
- can feel reassured by the dedication and hard work of the police team
- may enjoy seeing the police team's personal lives and the ways their dedication to policing interferes with their relationships
- may enjoy the humour, action and suspense.

Surveillance:
- the **social realism** offers a sense of informing the audience about police work and the criminal world.

Scheduling and *The Avengers*

In 1965 only three television channels were available – BBC One, BBC Two and ITV. There was no broadcasting for large parts of the day and all television channels closed down at night (playing the National Anthem). Televisions were black and white; colour television was not available until 1966. There were no remote controls – viewers had to get up to change channels on the set itself. With only three channels to choose from, audiences were much more loyal to particular channels.

The Avengers was scheduled in 1965 on ITV on Saturdays at 9.05 pm. This was peak viewing time, as *The Avengers* was a well-established, light-hearted spy thriller, which was expected to attract a mass audience. The fourth series attracted audiences of around 7 million homes, with episodes often appearing in the top ten television programmes.

Competition and *The Avengers*

There was fierce competition between the BBC and ITV, but ITV was financially secure as it was the only television channel to broadcast moving-image advertisements. The advertising revenue meant that ITV could afford bigger budgets than the BBC. ITV was controlled by the Independent Television Authority and made up of a network of television companies that competed with one another to provide programmes. *The Avengers* was produced by ABC, the ITV company responsible for weekend broadcasting for the Midlands and the North.

High production values

The fourth series of *The Avengers* had an additional injection of money from the American Broadcasting Company, giving each episode high production values. There could be more location shooting than in the previous three series and all episodes were to be shot on film. Each episode had a budget of around £56,000. For comparison, *The Ipcress File* – a major British spy film from the same year starring Michael Caine – had the relatively small production budget of £309,000.

> **Social realism:** a style of drama that is grounded in the contemporary world in terms of setting, characters and social issues, often portraying social injustice.

Revision activity
Using your study of *The Avengers*, add three more ways to the list below in which the programme specifically targeted its audience.

Elements of comedy combined with an exciting spy thriller
Sophisticated camerawork and editing
A range of interesting locations
A strong, intelligent, attractive female protagonist – Emma Peel

Why might 1960s audiences watch *The Avengers*?

How to use theory

Uses and Gratifications and *The Avengers*

Consider the four ways, identified by Blumler and Katz, in which audiences might use media products and gain pleasure from them.
Personal identity – audiences:

- could identify and empathise with upper-class role models
- could explore and/or reinforce their own views and values
- could identify with a cool, calm, unruffled English gentleman – Steed.
- could identify with a tough, intelligent, 'Swinging London' female hero, who was the equal of Steed – Emma Peel.

Social interaction and integration – audiences:

- could watch the programme together as family, as there was only one television in the house (apart from younger children as the programme was post-watershed)
- would enjoy discussing the programme – friends and co-workers would feel left out if they had not seen it
- could build a personal relationship with the familiar characters of Steed and Emma Peel – forgiving their weaknesses, admiring their achievements – almost as a substitute for real-life interaction
- in Britain and in other countries (the series had an international following) gained a sense of Britishness from *The Avengers*.

Entertainment – audiences:

- could enjoy the escapist plots
- could de-stress by losing themselves in the fantasy world of *The Avengers*
- could enjoy the jeopardy of their heroes' situations and how they escaped from these with style, sophistication and humour
- could enjoy the repetition and difference in the narrative, with a new villain each week and the familiar closure of Steed and Emma Peel driving away from the scene of their triumph.

Surveillance – audiences:

- could feel that they were gaining information about the world of the upper classes
- could feel that they were gaining information about the world from spy dramas – espionage was a frequent subject in the news
- could feel reassured by the idea that Steed and Emma Peel represented highly capable agents defending Britain from a foreign threat, despite the elements of **pastiche** rather than social realism.

Changing audience responses: *The Avengers*

Audiences watching *The Avengers* today might have very different responses to those of audiences watching the series in the 1960s. They might experience different pleasures or they might feel alienated from the series. A number of factors come into play:

- changes in social attitudes and values
- changes in performance style
- changes in production techniques, such as the use of black and white, the style of camerawork and the use of non-diegetic music
- personal experiences that shape our lives
- the cult status of *The Avengers*, supported by fansites.

Read the following example question and then the sample answer and the assessment comment that follow.

> **Pastiche**: a media product that imitates another product through visual style, media language or narrative.

Exam practice

Question 4

Describe what is meant by Public Service Broadcasting (PSB). Use the BBC as an example in your answer.

[5]

Example 1

The BBC is a public service broadcaster because it educates, entertains and informs. This means it will include news updates, regular television shows such as game shows, soap operas or talent shows, and documentaries such as *Planet Earth*.

The BBC is a very well-known British broadcaster because of its purposes and content.

The candidate has used some terms correctly but has not given enough detail on the BBC's public purposes. They have shown an understanding of the BBC's requirement to broadcast a range of diverse programmes, but they have not mentioned Ofcom and the way it regulates television. The answer displays adequate knowledge and understanding of PSB, placing it in Level 2.

Now time yourself to see whether you can produce a better answer in five minutes. Then take a look at this sample exam answer:

Example 2

The BBC, ITV, Channel 4, Channel 5 and S4C are the main PSB channels in the UK. Ofcom controls broadcasting in the UK and gives each channel their own requirements that they must meet in order to carry on broadcasting. The BBC has been a PSB channel since 1922, with Lord Reith stating that it must educate, inform and entertain.

Ofcom also says that the BBC must be distinctive – different from other channels – and represent and reflect diversity while attracting a mass audience. The BBC tries to do this with a range of different programmes – news and documentaries like *Blue Planet*, competitions like *Strictly Come Dancing* and drama series like *Cuffs*. *Cuffs* has a multicultural cast with older and younger characters to attract a mass audience and reflect diversity.

This is a better answer than the first one, as it demonstrates a very good understanding of PSB. It discusses the role of Ofcom and a number of the public purposes of the BBC, giving examples to support the points made. This makes it a strong Level 3 answer.

Now test yourself

1 Which of the following is a requirement of Public Service Broadcasting? Tick all that apply.

a To make distinctive programmes		
b To make money for shareholders		
c To stimulate knowledge and learning		
d To offer a lot of repeat broadcasts		
e To inform the public		
f To offer high-quality programmes		

2 List the four audience uses and gratifications as defined by Blumler and Katz.
3 Name the organisation that measures television audience ratings.
4 What is meant by a niche audience?
5 Name the organisation that regulates television in the UK.
6 How is the BBC funded?
7 List five media platforms that audiences can use to access television today.
8 Give two reasons why audiences might watch live television.

Answers on p. 132

How to prepare for the exam

- Remember that this question is about your knowledge and understanding of television, with the main focus on industries and audiences.
- You need to memorise a number of facts and key terms.
- Try using different-coloured cards for revision of television industries, television audiences and key terms.
- Note down the key points for each and ask a friend or member of your family to test you.

Question 5

What this question involves

Question 5 is worth 10 marks and will test your knowledge and understanding of the influence of contexts on television. The question focuses on the ways in which social, cultural, historical and contemporary attitudes and values affect television programmes. It could ask about:

- the influence of historical contexts on television, using *The Avengers* as an example
- the influence of contemporary contexts on television, using *Cuffs* as an example
- the influence of both historical and contemporary contexts on television, using both *Cuffs* and *The Avengers* as examples.

Timing

You should spend around ten minutes on this question. Your answer should be a short essay.

> **Exam tip**
>
> Remember that there are only 10 marks available, so make sure you make your points without a lengthy introduction.

What the examiner is looking for

REVISED

Examiners are looking for knowledge and understanding of the media contexts of *Cuffs* and/or *The Avengers*, and how the relevant media contexts are reflected in *Cuffs* and/or *The Avengers*.

The student should produce either a detailed description of one context with a sophisticated explanation of how it influences programmes with reference to *Cuffs* and/or *The Avengers* or an effective description of a number of social contexts with an explanation of their influence on *Cuffs* and/or *The Avengers*.

For this question you will revise:
- the specific episodes you have studied – *Cuffs*, Series 1, Episode 1, BBC One and *The Avengers*, Series 4, Episode 1, ITV
- the overall format of the *Cuffs* series (as a pre-watershed police procedural drama with comic elements) and the overall format of the fourth series of *The Avengers* (as a light-hearted spy thriller)
- the social and cultural context of the mid-1960s with reference to *The Avengers*, focusing on
  - concerns over the **Cold War**
  - changing attitudes to gender roles
  - changing attitudes to sexuality
  - changing attitudes to class
  - changing attitudes to age – 'the generation gap'
  - ethnicity
- the social and cultural context of 2015 with reference to *Cuffs*, focusing on
  - changing attitudes to gender roles
  - changing attitudes to sexualities
  - **multiculturalism**
  - age
  - changing attitudes towards the police.

> **Cold War**: the state of hostility that existed between the Soviet bloc and the Western powers from c1947 to 1991.
>
> **Multiculturalism**: the change from a white society in which racism is 'normal' to one characterised by many different racial and ethnic groups.

Social and cultural contexts of the mid-1960s

REVISED

Key moments 1961–1965

This timeline gives you an idea of the political and cultural background of the first half of the 1960s. The films mentioned here were all big box office hits (apart from *The War Game*, which was censored), reflecting changing attitudes in society and British concerns about spying and the nuclear threat during that period.

1961 The Berlin Wall is built, symbolising the Cold War between the Soviet bloc and the West; J F Kennedy becomes US president; *The Avengers* begins on BBC.

1962 The Cuban missile crisis; *Dr No* (the first James Bond film); the Beatles' first record, 'Love Me Do'; *The Saint* begins on ITV (mystery spy thriller starring Roger Moore); the Pilkington Report criticises the populism of ITV and recommends that the BBC is awarded the third channel, BBC Two.

> **Exam tip**
>
> You do not need to learn all of these facts, but mentioning one or two of them in relation to *The Avengers* may help you to gain marks.

1963 *From Russia With Love* (the second James Bond film); Mary Whitehouse begins 'Clean Up TV' campaign; J F Kennedy assassinated in Dallas; Martin Luther King's speech, 'I have a dream'.

1964 Nelson Mandela jailed for life; BBC Two begins broadcasting; Labour wins the general election; *Goldfinger* (the third James Bond film); *Carry on Spying* (a parody of more serious spy films, especially the Bond films); the Beatles' film *A Hard Day's Night*.

1965 *The Ipcress File* (an unglamorous spy film with Michael Caine as a British agent); *Thunderball* (the fourth James Bond film); *The Spy Who Came in from the Cold* (a Cold War spy film); *The War Game* (a fiction film on the effects of a nuclear attack on Britain); *It Happened Here* (a fiction film depicting the occupation of Britain by the Nazis); *The Man From U.N.C.L.E.* (American spy thriller TV series) first broadcast on BBC One; the Race Relations Act passed (the first UK law to outlaw racial discrimination).

Revision activity

Identify four more facts from the timeline that have an influence on *The Avengers*, Series 4, Episode 1, ITV: 'The Town of No Return'. Note them in the table below.

Timeline fact	Influence seen in 'The Town of No Return'
It Happened Here (1965), a fiction film documenting the occupation of Britain by the Nazis – this referred to the past, but referenced the fear of invasion and occupation in 1965.	The theme of the episode is the planned invasion of Britain by an unspecified Eastern bloc army, supported by **fifth columnists**.

Concerns over the Cold War

In 1965 the Cold War (c1947–1991) was at its height. Britain was a member of NATO (the North Atlantic Treaty Organization), a group of 12 western countries, including the USA, which agreed to support one another in the face of an attack from the Soviet Union. In retaliation the Soviet Union formed the Warsaw Pact in 1955 with seven other communist countries. From 1955 Europe was divided into two armed camps, NATO and the Warsaw Pact.

> **Fifth columnists**: a group of people who secretly support the enemy and undermine a country from within.

The threat of nuclear war

Anxieties about nuclear war were common, as both the Soviet Union and the USA were building up their armies and weapons, which included the nuclear bomb. In 1962 the Cuban Missile Crisis took place over a terrifying seven days, when the Soviet Union and the USA brought the world to the brink of nuclear war.

Espionage

Both sides in the Cold War used espionage – spying – as a way of finding out what the other was doing through secret operations or spreading false knowledge. A number of double agents were found guilty of spying in the early 1960s and either defected to the Soviet Union or were imprisoned. This meant that espionage was a common theme in films like *From Russia With Love* (1963), and television programmes like *The Man from U.N.C.L.E.* (1964–1968) and *The Avengers* (1961–1969).

Revision activity

Find out more about spying during the Cold War on this site: www.historylearningsite.co.uk/modern-world-history-1918-to-1980/the-cold-war/spies-of-the-cold-war-era/

How did concerns over the Cold War and spying influence 'The Town of No Return'?

The opening sequence of 'The Town of No Return' symbolises the theme of the episode, which can be summed up as the attempted invasion of Britain supported by 'the enemy within'. Saul, who apparently represents the stereotypical British fisherman, is not alarmed by the strange arrival of the impostor Mark Brandon from the sea in a waterproof bag, but directs the invader to Lower Bazeley as if a smartly dressed 'English gentleman' wading in from the sea were an everyday occurrence. This alerts the 1965 audience to familiar themes linked to spying: disguise and impersonation.

Intertextual references

As the episode continues, the 1965 audience would have quickly understood that the town of Little Bazeley is under threat from fifth columnists, referencing World War II films such as *Went the Day Well?* from 1944. The sleepy English country village of Lower Bazeley offers an **intertextual reference** to the quiet Oxfordshire village of Little Bramley from the 1944 film *Went the Day Well?*. In both cases the English country village is an illusion, as sinister intruders are impersonating stereotypical British characters. Audiences in 1965 would have made the connections with the Cold War threat from the Soviet Union.

Intertextual references: references to other media products that are expected to be recognised by the audience.

Element of pastiche

As the format of the series is a light-hearted spy thriller, the representation of 'the enemy within' is not seriously threatening. Terence Alexander, who plays impostor landlord Piggy Warren, was well known in 1965 as a comic actor of film and television, who often played the charming villain. His performance, together with his oversized handlebar moustache, plays down the potentially sinister element of threat. This would fit with the audience's need for reassurance that while the threat existed, the enemy was not efficient enough to succeed.

Reassuring the audience

The sequence in which Emma Peel uses the blackboard to explain the planned invasion of Britain to Steed is a playful intertextual reference to the planning sequence in the 1955 film *The Dam Busters*. The lightness of the dialogue and the short amount of **screen time** given to this important exposition, together with the fact that Steed sits behind a child's desk, serve to reassure the audience that the threat is not as significant as the threat of invasion was in the early years of World War II.

Screen time: the amount of time a character is given in a programme; lead characters are given more time than supporting characters.

The cool, calm and ironic response to danger shown by Steed and Emma also helps to undercut the threat and reassure the audience at a time of some national anxiety that they are safe with secret agents like Steed and Emma to protect them.

Concerns about the threat posed by the Cold War are reflected in 'The Town of No Return'. This episode of *The Avengers* seeks to reassure the audience and minimise the threat. Identify some key moments in the episode to illustrate the techniques used to reassure the audience:

Technique	Example
References to World War II	The sequence when Steed walks around the deserted airfield, plays on the roundabout and doffs his hat to his reflection in the broken mirror is a salute to all those involved in World War II and reminds the audience that Britain triumphed.
Humour	As Emma alerts Steed to the fact she has been tied up in the blacksmith's forge, the dialogue is comic and playful: 'Tight girth', 'Cut down on the oats'.
Editing	The editing does not allow the audience to dwell on the murdered Smallwood or on the dying Mark Brandon. This lack of screen time makes these moments less significant in the narrative.
Melodrama	
Casting and performance	
Commitment to duty	
Representation of the enemy	

How did changing attitudes towards gender roles in 1965 influence 'The Town of No Return'?

A new breed of tough, intelligent women

Not everyone in Britain in 1965 supported the idea of women taking on more dominant roles in society and popular culture. There was criticism of working mothers, who were often blamed for the disruption of family life. These opposing attitudes are clearly reflected in the representation of Emma Peel in 'The Town of No Return'.

The episode was the first appearance of Diana Rigg as Emma Peel. For the first three series, Steed's assistant had been Dr Cathy Gale, an anthropologist who was skilled at judo. When Honor Blackman left the series to appear in the Bond film *Goldfinger*, Diana Rigg continued the tradition of intelligent, physically tough women in *The Avengers* with her character, Mrs Emma Peel.

Sex objects

However, in both cases, these positive representations of women are undercut by the fact that they are sexually objectified, in particular by their leather catsuits. The camerawork also reinforces the sexual objectification, with a close-up of Emma Peel's bottom as Steed pats it with his foil during the introductory fencing match in 'The Town of No Return'.

Emma's name was thought up because Steed's new assistant had to have M(an) Appeal – Emma Peel. So, on the one hand audiences were presented with a breakthrough representation of women in the highly intelligent martial arts expert Emma Peel. On the other hand, this was a stereotypical representation of women as Emma was subordinate to Steed and sexually objectified.

Ideological tension in 1965

The apparent contradiction between the representation of Emma as an equal to Steed and her sexual objectification is a very good example of the influence of the social and cultural contexts on 'The Town of No Return'. These contradictions reflect the **ideological tension** between shifting attitudes towards women and their actual roles in society in the mid-1960s.

Far more women were going to university and pursuing professional roles in 1965. But women were still not guaranteed equal pay for doing the same job as a man; the Equal Pay Act was not passed until 1970. Women did not have control over their fertility, as although the contraceptive pill was available, this was for married women only.

> **Ideological tension**: opposing values, ideas and beliefs.
>
> **Anti-stereotype**: a portrayal of a member of a social group, place, event or issue that goes against the generally accepted stereotype.
>
> **Reactionary**: opposing social progress and change.
>
> **Stereotype**: an oversimplified portrayal of a member of a social group, place, event or issue, which is based on assumptions.

Revision activity

Identify more key moments in 'The Town of No Return' where Emma Peel is represented as an **anti-stereotype** or where she is represented as a **reactionary stereotype**.

Emma Peel as an anti-stereotype	Emma Peel as a reactionary stereotype
Emma overpowers Steed in the fencing match (though he later overpowers her by cheating and fighting 'dirty')	Emma is ordered by Steed to leave immediately for Lower Bazeley on a mission, without warning
Emma acts as the dominant schoolmistress as she explains the enemy plot to Steed, who sits behind a child's desk in the schoolroom	Emma becomes the Proppian 'princess' figure waiting to be rescued by hero Steed after she has been tied up in the sexually suggestive saddle with a 'tight girth'
Emma never shows fear but is always brimming with self-confidence – even when she is outnumbered by the impostors Brandon and Saul after overpowering the vicar	Emma admires Steed's ability to overcome Brandon and four enemy soldiers – in comparison to her victory over one woman and a vicar

Find out more about the history of gender equality by reading some of these resources:
- www.bl.uk/sisterhood/teaching-resources
- www.mmu.ac.uk/equality-and-diversity/doc/gender-equality-timeline.pdf

---

How did changing attitudes towards sexuality in 1965 influence 'The Town of No Return'?

Emma is confident in her sexuality and is an equal partner to Steed in any suggestion of a romantic involvement. This reflects the social changes in attitudes towards sexual behaviour. Those who supported the 'permissive society' of the 1960s did not condemn sex outside marriage. Despite the suggestions, Emma and Steed are never seen to engage in a sexual relationship on screen, perhaps reflecting a more traditional approach to relationships than seen in many other media products of the time, such as the Bond films.

In 'The Town of No Return' there is an assumption that everyone is heterosexual. This was the 'norm' for most television programmes in the 1960s and reflects the marginalisation of LGBT groups before gay liberation and changes in the law.

How did changing attitudes towards class in 1965 influence 'The Town of No Return'?

In the 1960s full employment had improved the standard of living, although class divisions were still clear. Working-class people could afford cars and televisions, and attitudes shifted from the idea of culture as something that belonged to an educated minority towards popular culture that was available for all. At the same time, London became the centre of some exciting trends in fashion, music and art, and the idea of London as 'swinging' developed (although this term was not used until 1966 by *Time* magazine).

In 'The Town of No Return' Steed and Emma are upper-class characters. Both are privately educated and speak with received pronunciation and upper-class accents. Steed represents the upper class of the past with his bowler and brolly, while Emma represents the youth of 'swinging London', where class divisions were less apparent.

Steed and Emma travel from London to Little Bazeley in a first-class carriage, with Steed producing from his carpet bag a silver teapot and a three-tiered cake stand for afternoon tea. The sequence is presented ironically and is not intended to be taken seriously. This would help audiences to continue to identify with the characters rather than feel alienated from them through class differences.

> **Revision activity**
>
> Find out more about the 1960s by using the national archive resources at www.nationalarchives.gov.uk/education/resources/sixties-britain/
> Make notes from these on attitudes towards the Cold War, gender and class.

How did changing attitudes towards age in 1965 influence 'The Town of No Return'?

There was a strong focus on youth in fashion, music and entertainment, which reflected changing social attitudes and values in the decade. Not everyone welcomed this, however; many members of the older generation put up strong resistance to the changing attitudes.

These differences in attitudes and values became known as the 'generation gap'. This generation gap is cleverly dealt with in 'The Town of No Return' through the use of the two protagonists. Steed represents the values of the older generation, having fought in the war, while Emma represents the values of 'swinging London'. Rather than clashing, the two complement each other, with Steed's polite English gentleman working perfectly with Emma's vibrant, 'swinging sixties' young woman.

If you look at the table, you can see how the producers managed to accommodate both sets of values in the two protagonists in this episode of *The Avengers*.

Steed – the older generation	Emma – the younger generation
Bowler hat – symbol of a British 'City' gentleman but Steed's is reinforced with steel and used to overcome the enemy in the underground bunker at the end of the episode.	Op art black and white beret – symbol of 'swinging London' and the cutting edge of fashion. Used as an ornament and to increase Emma's attractiveness.
Black umbrella – symbol of a British 'City gentleman' but is also used as an effective weapon against the impostor Piggy Warren.	Black leather catsuit, donned by Emma once she realises that the village has been taken over by the enemy – ostensibly to make fighting easier, but at the same time displaying her curvaceous body and objectifying her (in fact, Diana Rigg hated wearing leather and jersey catsuits were later designed for her by John Bates).
Expensive, bespoke three-piece suit, reinforcing the idea that Steed is part of the Establishment.	Mini skirt – seen as the symbol of the 'swinging sixties' liberated young woman, but not practical, especially not in a fight.
Steed gains respect from the older generation for having fought in World War II and pays homage to those who fought in the war in the deserted airfield sequence – this reflects duty to Queen and country (Patrick Macnee was a naval officer during the war).	Emma represents the more youthful, carefree individualism of 'swinging London'. Nevertheless, she too shows a commitment to duty in the way she joins Steed on the mission without complaint (he has already bought two train tickets, leaving her without a choice).
Steed always refers to Emma as 'Mrs Peel' and behaves towards her in a courteous, flirtatious way.	Emma is always polite and correct in her choice of language, and behaves in a cool, flirtatious way with Steed.

How did attitudes towards ethnicity in 1965 influence 'The Town of No Return'?

There were very few black or Asian actors on television in the 1960s. Former colonies such as Zimbabwe were still struggling to gain independence from Britain. As support for these countries and for the anti-apartheid movement in South Africa and Civil Rights in the USA developed, this was reflected by a slow increase in the representation of different cultural groups in popular culture.

The Race Relations Act against racial discrimination was passed in 1965, but racial and ethnic inequalities in society remained. This was reflected in television programmes like 'The Town of No Return', in which the cast is all-white (typical of *The Avengers* and of drama series of the time as a whole).

> **Exam tip**
>
> Remember that you can use some of the points made in the section in Question 4 on audience uses and gratifications and *The Avengers* to answer Question 5 in the exam.

Exam practice

Question 5

Explain how social contexts influence television programmes. Refer to *The Avengers* from 1965 to support your answer.

[10]

Example 1

Social contexts influence television programmes for lots of reasons. Gender is one of these reasons. In the swinging sixties women wore mini-skirts and there was the permissive society. Emma Peel in *The Avengers* wears a mini-skirt and a leather catsuit, showing that the programme was made in the swinging sixties. As women were able to be stronger in the 1960s, she is good at fighting and beats the vicar and the schoolteacher in a fight.

Other things that influenced *The Avengers* were spying, the Cold War and the generation gap.

The student focuses on gender and shows adequate knowledge and understanding of media contexts and their effects on programmes. They mention some of the other ways in which social contexts influence television programmes. However, the answer is brief and underdeveloped, placing it in Level 2 and gaining 4–5 marks.

Now time yourself to see if you can produce a better answer in ten minutes. Then take a look at Example 2.

Example 2

In 'The Town of No Return' (TTONR) we can see the influence of social contexts very clearly. In 1965 audiences were fearful of an attack from the Soviet Union, as they remembered the Cuban Missile Crisis of 1962, when the USA and the Soviet Union had nearly begun a nuclear war. This is reflected in TTONR as the storyline is a planned invasion of Britain by an enemy who kill off all the inhabitants of Little Bazeley and then pretend to be them. They bring in soldiers from submarines or ships a few at a time and keep them in the underground bunkers.

Audiences in 1965 would feel comforted by the fact that Emma Peel and Steed are able to work out what is going on very quickly and defeat the enemy in an easy fight (Steed wipes out four enemy soldiers with his bowler hat) before they have managed to carry out their plan. This suggests to the audience that the government has many intelligent secret agents like Emma and Steed to protect the British people.

Another way that social contexts influence *The Avengers* is in the representation of gender. The 'swinging sixties' saw big changes in the ways that women behaved and Emma represents this with her confident, cool behaviour (she never looks scared, even when she is cornered by Brandon and Saul), and her mini-skirts and leather catsuits show her to be a 'liberated' young woman (even though they make her into a sex object). She is a scientist and a martial arts expert and wins her fights with the impostor vicar and the headmistress, Jill Manson.

Steed represents the traditional English gentleman who is physically strong, clever and very polite. Although he is more old-fashioned than Emma, he works well as a team with her. This shows you how *The Avengers* reflected the social contexts of the 1960s.

This is a much better response, displaying excellent knowledge and understanding of contexts and their effects on *The Avengers*. The student discusses two social contexts, the Cold War and changing attitudes towards gender, and gives detailed examples from 'The Town of No Return' to support the points made. This places the answer in the top Level 3, giving the student 10 marks.

Now test yourself

TESTED

1 Identify one way in which concerns over the Cold War influenced 'The Town of No Return'.
2 Why did so many films and television programmes in the 1960s use spying as a theme?
3 What is a fifth columnist?
4 When was the Equal Pay Act introduced?
5 What did Steed do during World War II?
6 How did the writers of *The Avengers* think of the name for Steed's new assistant?
7 How does Steed find out that Piggy Warren is an impostor?
8 What was the 'generation gap'?

Answers on p. 132

Social and cultural contexts of 2015

REVISED

Introduction

In the 50 years between 'The Town of No Return' and *Cuffs*, Series 1, Episode 1, 'Luck of the Draw', there were huge changes in social and cultural contexts. A number of laws were passed to make discrimination against people because of their gender, race, disability and sexuality illegal. These laws were clarified and combined in the Equality Act of 2010. These changes in social attitudes and values meant that by 2015 television audiences had become familiar with a diversity of representations in their television programmes.

How did changing attitudes towards gender roles in 2015 influence *Cuffs*, Episode 1?

Changing attitudes towards women

The Women's Liberation Movement, which began in 1970, helped to shape important changes for women in Britain, particularly to do with equality in education and job opportunities. Many improvements in gender equality have taken place, but the 'fourth wave' feminists of today would argue that women still have to deal with discrimination and prejudice, together with a gender pay gap, despite legislation.

Since the 2000s stronger roles for women have been developed in series such as *Holby City* and dramas like *Dr Foster*, sometimes at the expense of strong roles for males. The ensemble cast of *Cuffs* attempts to give equal status to men and women and to fit the BBC's remit to reflect the culture and values of the UK.

Let's look at how social and cultural contexts influence women's roles in *Cuffs*.

Women's roles and representations in *Cuffs*, Episode 1	
DS Jo Moffat	Jo has important status as an investigator, although it could be argued that her independence is weakened by her affair with her superior, Chief Superintendent Robert Vickers. She is represented as weak when she hesitates about leading the press conference on the racist attack, but is represented as strong when she orders the police raid on the party in order to arrest the racist criminals. Jo has power because of her status in the police force, reflecting the number of women in positions of authority in 2015.
PC Donna Prager	Donna is represented as physically and mentally stronger than her police partner, Lino. She is kind to Lino, despite his failings. Donna is equal to Ryan during training, and she keeps going when Lino and Jake have given up. This reflects social attitudes in 2015, with many women valuing both mental and physical fitness.
PC Misha Baig	Represented as fairly weak in this episode, when she is unprepared for the ram-raid in the town centre, Misha is used as a contrast to Donna, as she is younger and more inexperienced.
Debbie Vickers	Debbie is suffering from cancer and her husband, Superintendent Vickers, is having an affair with DS Jo Moffat. Her representation is fairly stereotypical, but Debbie's traditional maternal role gives her power in this episode.

Changing attitudes towards masculinity

Changes in social attitudes towards masculinity have meant that men are no longer confined to traditional male roles in television drama series. Strength is not always equated to physicality and there are many positive representations of men in caring roles once reserved for women. Contemporary debates about gender identity have helped audiences to accept these different versions of masculinity.

The influence of changes in attitudes towards masculinity in the 2010s can be seen in *Cuffs'* attempt to represent a range of types of masculinity in a positive light. Have a look at the table to help you consider the different male roles in *Cuffs*.

Men's roles and representations in *Cuffs*, Episode 1	
PC Jake Vickers	As the son of the superintendent, Jake has been taken onto the police force without completing all the required training. This apparent favouritism makes him unpopular with his fellow police officers and results in him making a number of mistakes. He does not initially display many traditional male qualities of physical and mental strength, representing him as weak and lacking in dedication. However, a plot device allows Jake to prove himself as physically tough and to display traditional masculine qualities when he saves Ryan from a knife attack.
Chief Superintendent Robert Vickers	This is a more traditional representation of masculinity, with Vickers taking on the role of the dominant, controlling male whose job is to keep his team of detectives and police officers in line.
PC Lino Moretti	Lino is the weaker character in the police partnership with Donna, with his lack of physical athleticism and his pleasure in food providing humour. Lino is not a very positive representation of masculinity in this episode as he takes on a childlike role.
DC Carl Hawkins	Carl is a sympathetic representation of a male who finds the struggle of trying for another child with his wife difficult. This shows the influence of social contexts, as fertility was debated openly in 2015, although it is anti-stereotypical that the issue is dealt with from a male point of view in a television drama.

PC Ryan Draper and masculinity

The most interesting and developed representation of masculinity is seen in Ryan Draper.

- Traditionally 'masculine' qualities: Ryan's experience and the fact that he is respected by his fellow police and trusted by Robert Vickers to mentor his son, Jake, mean that he is given a great deal of power. He shows gritty determination during the car chase. He demonstrates complete commitment to duty when his lunch break is interrupted by the call for help after the ram-raid burglary, and he responds with courage and determination. His bravery, is shown when he, Jo and Carl confront the racist criminals. These are fairly stereotypical elements in traditional representations of masculinity.

- Traditionally 'feminine' qualities: at the same time, Ryan is gentle in his dealings with the public, treating the drug addict Nathan with kindness. He is represented as emotional, letting his anger get the better of him when he tells Jake off for giving the wrong instructions on the commentary and allowing the criminals to escape. As the widowed father of two children, he is represented as a caring parent, taking on a maternal role by brushing his daughter's hair and giving his son a hot drink while he does his homework (even though Ryan had earlier caught him out of school practising parkour).

- A multi-dimensional character: this multi-dimensional combination of qualities offers an interesting representation of masculinity, which reflects the influence of social attitudes and values in 2015. Most importantly, the masculine and feminine qualities in Ryan combine to allow him to act as a symbol for the dedication of the police in a tough world.

Revision activity

Find two adjectives to describe the types of masculinity represented by the male characters in *Cuffs* and decide whether these representations are stereotypical or anti-stereotypical.

Character	Type of masculinity	Stereotypical or anti-stereotypical?
Chief Superintendent Robert Vickers	Authoritative Patriarchal	Stereotypical
PC Jake Vickers		
Station Inspector Graham Webb		
PC Lino Moretti		
DC Carl Hawkins		
DI Felix Kane		

How did changing attitudes towards sexualities in 2015 influence 'Luck of the Draw'?

The Equality Act of 2010 made discrimination against LGBT people illegal. By 2015 audiences were used to seeing gay characters on pre-watershed television programmes such as *EastEnders* and *Holby City*. This increase in the visibility of LGBT characters in 2015 reflects the fact that the BBC had confidence that audiences would accept representations of gay characters' personal lives, just as they accepted the heterosexual characters' personal lives in programmes like *Cuffs*.

Challenging the stereotype

The introductory episode of *Cuffs* challenges the stereotype of a character's sexuality being represented as a problem. Within the first ten minutes of the episode Jake makes it clear to Ryan and the audience that he is openly gay, 22 and single. Jake's sexuality is not remarked upon nor seen as a problem; the problem for Ryan is that Jake is the boss's son. When the duty solicitor Simon Reddington shows an interest in Jake, Ryan is concerned – not about Jake's sexuality but because the solicitor is seen as creating obstacles for the police: Ryan advises Jake to distance himself from Simon.

Donna Prager is also a gay character, although this is not revealed until the end of Episode 2 when the audience sees a montage of the characters' evenings when off duty. Donna's relationship with her wife, artist Alice Gove, is presented equally with the heterosexual relationships of other characters.

A breakthrough representation?

These representations of gay characters are anti-stereotypical as they are non-judgemental and presented as part of the **social realist** style of *Cuffs*. This first episode is seen mainly through the eyes of Jake on his first day, with his character given many close-ups and the most screen time. Jake is represented as weak initially but he gains the respect of his colleagues and of the audience when he saves Ryan with a perfectly placed punch. This places the gay character centre stage, resulting in what could be argued is a breakthrough representation.

> **Social realist**: a style of drama that is grounded in the contemporary world in terms of setting, characters and social issues, often portraying social injustice.

How did attitudes towards multiculturalism in 2015 influence 'Luck of the Draw'?

By 2015 television audiences recognised that Britain was a multicultural society, despite political debates about immigration and the EU. This positive view of multiculturalism is strongly reflected in *Cuffs*, where there are a number of different ethnicities in the police team, but these are hardly remarked on or noticed. Just as Jake's homosexuality is accepted, so too is the fact that Donna is half Japanese, Lino is half Italian, Ryan is Black British and Misha is Asian. As long as the police work together as a team, differences are accepted.

Challenge to racism

Despite the Equality Act of 2010, racism in Britain still exists and this is reflected in 'Luck of the Draw', where one of the main themes is racism. The first serious crime featured in the episode is the unprovoked racist attack on the young Asian, Amit, by a gang of four white racist men. The representation of the racist group as an underclass of aggressive, poorly educated, beer-swilling thugs is intentionally stereotypical – the audience is intended to be alienated from them. The violent, cowardly attack on Amit, together with the contrasting representation of Amit as a kind, caring, gentle son, conveys a powerful anti-racist message, reflecting the social contexts of 2015.

How did attitudes towards age in 2015 influence 'Luck of the Draw'?

The main focus in this episode is on Jake, who at 22 is the youngest of the uniformed police team of 30-somethings. *Cuffs* aims to attract its audience through the energy and attractiveness of the relatively young police team of Ryan, Donna, Lino and Jake. The physical energy and dedication of the team are celebrated in the sequence when they train in the car park after a long day's work.

As *Cuffs* uses an ensemble cast, older characters such as Jo, Carl, Felix and Robert are also given storylines with complicated personal lives. This is an attempt by the BBC to appeal to a mass, diverse audience.

How did changing attitudes towards the police in 2015 influence 'Luck of the Draw'?

In 2015, social attitudes towards the police were not all positive. This was partly because of negative publicity over police corruption and cuts to police budgets, leading to some crimes not being investigated. Even if the public were not against the police, they lacked confidence in them. This attitude is illustrated by the male nudist in the teaser to 'Luck of the Draw' with his dismissive attitude towards Ryan's attempts to help.

Cuffs challenges this negative view of the police by offering a set of values for the audience to admire and respect:
- dedication to duty, sometimes at the expense of their private lives
- commitment to the job, despite being overworked and undervalued
- the ability to work as a team – comradeship
- kindness and compassion
- moral integrity
- physical and mental strength
- endurance
- resilience.

> **Revision activity**
>
> Using this list, see whether you can find an example to illustrate each of the values in 'Luck of the Draw'.

> **Exam tip**
>
> Remember that you can use some of the points made in the section in Question 4 on audience uses and gratifications and *Cuffs* to answer Question 5 in the exam.

Exam practice

Question 5

Explain how social contexts influence television programmes. Refer to *Cuffs* from 2015 to support your answer.   [10]

Key differences between representations in the two programmes

A good way of revising both programmes is to draw up some tables that compare the key areas covered above. This will also help you to be prepared for a question that asks you how social contexts influence both programmes. On the next page you will find an example for you to follow.

Representation of gender	
'The Town of No Return', 1965	**'Luck of the Draw', 2015**
Emma is sexually objectified through her codes of dress and the camerawork.	Jo and Donna wear masculinised codes of dress and are not sexually objectified.
Emma is Steed's assistant and is told by him that she is going on a mission to Little Bazeley, almost as an order.	Jo is in control of DC Carl Hawkins and of the uniformed police; she orders the police raid on the party even though they are outnumbered. However, she is subordinate to CS Robert Vickers.
Emma wins the fight with the vicar in the church but is overcome by Saul and Brandon.	Jo wins the fight with the racist at the party and arrests him.
Emma and Steed are successful because they use their individual masculine and feminine skills to work together as a team.	The police are most successful when they work together as a team (where gender roles are not as significant as in 1965).
Steed rarely displays his emotions, but stays cool and witty whatever life throws at him.	Ryan's emotions are always near the surface. He displays heroic qualities but is able to show his 'feminine' side.

Now answer the question below. Use the material from your completed grid and remember that you only have ten minutes, so it will be sensible to pick one area of representation in order to have time to write about both programmes.

Exam practice

Question 5

How do television programmes reflect different historical contexts? Use *The Avengers*, 'The Town of No Return', and *Cuffs*, 'Luck of the Draw', to illustrate your answer. [10]

Now test yourself

TESTED ☐

9 What was the purpose of the Equality Act of 2010?
10 Write down three words to describe the representation of Chief Superintendent Robert Vickers in 'Luck of the Draw'.
11 Is the representation of Chief Superintendent Robert Vickers stereotypical or anti-stereotypical?
12 Give an example of an anti-stereotype of sexuality in 'Luck of the Draw'.
13 Give one way in which social contexts influenced the representation of women in 'Luck of the Draw'.
14 Give one way in which social contexts influenced the representation of masculinity in 'Luck of the Draw'.
15 Give one way in which social contexts influenced the representation of the police in 'Luck of the Draw'.

Answers on p. 132

How to prepare for the exam

- Watch both set episodes – 'The Town of No Return' and 'Luck of the Draw' – again.
- Select three key sequences from each episode that show the influence of social and cultural contexts.
- Make brief notes on these and learn them for the exam.
- Go over the key points on the social and cultural contexts of the 1960s and of 2015.
- Revise 'The Town of No Return' under the following headings: the Cold War, gender, sexuality, class, age, ethnicity.
- Revise 'Luck of the Draw' under the following headings: gender, sexuality, ethnicity, age, attitudes towards the police.

Paper 1 – Section B: Promoting Media

Media **promotion** is a crucial part of the industry. If a product is not marketed effectively, it cannot reach its target audience and therefore cannot hope to make the one thing the media industry seeks: profit.

One example of highly effective media promotion is the way *The Lego Movie* **franchise** (2014) marketed its products across a range of media forms. You will be asked about the following set media products, all relating to this franchise:

- film – *The Lego Movie* (Warner Bros, 2014)
- advertising – the film trailer and posters used to promote *The Lego Movie*
- video games – *The Lego Movie* video game (developed by TT Fusion, 2014).

> **Promotion**: the way in which a media product is marketed and 'sold' to an audience.
>
> **Franchise**: a collection of media products (e.g. films, television programmes, video games) all based on an original creative work. For example, the *Star Wars* series of films and related media is one of the most well-known and successful franchises in history.

Which areas of the theoretical framework must I study?	
Media language	You may be asked to consider the way promotional materials have been constructed, thinking about aspects such as mise-en-scène.
Media representation	You may be asked to respond to how issues such as gender, ethnicity and age are represented in the promotion of *The Lego Movie* or *The Lego Movie* video game.
Media audiences	You may be asked to consider how audiences are targeted by the franchise, and the different ways they respond to and interact with the products.
Media industries	You will be asked to think about how the franchise operates across different areas of the media industry, and the ways those industries often work together.

The four questions in this section will be as follows:

Question 6	1 mark	Will likely ask for knowledge of film, advertising or video games and be a fact-based question. Should be a very short answer.
Question 7	4 marks	Will likely ask for knowledge and understanding of film, advertising or video games from any area of the theoretical framework. Should be at least two sentences, taking about four minutes to answer.
Question 8	10 marks	Will likely ask for knowledge and understanding of film, advertising or video games from any area of the theoretical framework. Should be a short essay, taking about ten minutes to answer.
Question 9	10 marks	Will likely ask for analysis of media language or representation, focusing only on advertising or the video game, possibly in relation to their contexts. Should be a short essay, taking about ten minutes to answer.

Question 6

What this question involves

REVISED ☐

This is a 1-mark knowledge-only question about film, advertising or video games that is likely to be about media industries but could cover any area of the theoretical framework. You will not be asked a question about media language or representation in relation to studying the film industry.

Timing

This is a short question that should take less than one minute.

What the examiner is looking for

Examiners are looking for correct answers. The answer might be something such as a definition of a key term, a fact about the media industries, the name of a regulator.

Exam practice

Question 6

Which company produced and distributed *The Lego Movie*? [1]

For this question you will revise:
- factual questions, probably about media industries, but any area could come up in this question
- media industries facts for film, advertising and video games.

What do media regulators do?

Regulator	Industry		Example
BBFC (British Board of Film Classification)	Film	Classifies films and DVDs by giving an age rating based on their content.	*The Lego Movie* was given a 'U' rating by the BBFC.
VSC (Video Standards Council)	Video games	Classify video games by giving an age rating based on their content. They use the PEGI (Pan European Game Information) system to do this.	*The Lego Movie* video game was given a PEGI rating of 7+.
ASA (Advertising Standards Authority)	Advertising	Ensures the content of audio-visual and print advertising meets acceptable standards	In 2016, the ASA received 1,063 complaints about an advert for moneysupermarket.com due to content which some audiences found to be overtly sexual.

Revision activity

Go to the following websites and look at the regulatory information for both *The Lego Movie* and *The Lego Movie* video game: www.bbfc.co.uk and www.videostandards.org.uk
- Why did the BBFC give *The Lego Movie* a PG rating? What does this mean in terms of the audience the film can reach?
- Why did the VSC award a PEGI rating of 7+ to *The Lego Movie* video game?

Media institutions

REVISED

- Warner Bros produced and distributed *The Lego Movie*.
- TT Fusion produced *The Lego Movie* video game.

Now test yourself

TESTED

1 Which regulator is responsible for classifying films in the UK?
2 Which stage of the production process follows distribution?
3 What is meant by promotion?
4 Which company produced *The Lego Movie* video game?
5 Warner Bros is a media conglomerate. What does this mean?
6 A film that is designed to make large profits to support funding of others is known as what?
7 *The Lego Movie* can be defined as being part of a franchise. Why?

Answers on p. 132

Distribution: the stage of the production process when a product is made available to media audiences. This often also includes the promotion of the product.

Conglomerate: a large (often multinational) business organisation that owns a number of different companies.

How to prepare for the exam

- Ensure you revise all the key facts and definitions that we have covered in this section
- Test your knowledge of these key facts by doing revision activities such as making flash cards of the key information or asking questions with a friend.

Question 7

What this question involves

REVISED

Question 7 is a 4-mark knowledge and understanding question, which could be about film, advertising or video games (or a combination of these). It is likely to be about media industries but can cover any area of the theoretical framework, including media audiences. You will not be asked about media language, representation or audiences in relation to the film industry.

Timing

REVISED

Question 7 is a short question that should take about four minutes.

What the examiner is looking for

REVISED

Examiners are looking for answers that show knowledge and understanding of specific areas of the theoretical framework. You could be asked about any area of the theoretical framework regarding the way the film was promoted and your study of *The Lego Movie* video game.

You will not be asked a question regarding media language or representations in relation to the film itself.

Exam practice

Question 7

Explain two reasons why a film company would release a video game linked to a film. [4]

> There are several reasons why a film company would release a video game linked to a film. First, the promotion of the film is extended by the release of the video game. In the case of The Lego Movie franchise, the marketing of the film is helped by releasing a video game based on the film, especially on a platform that is popular with similar demographics.
>
> Second, this increase in promotion and synergy between different media sectors will help to ensure more profit is made overall. Warner Bros owns TT Fusion, who developed the Lego Movie video game, and therefore the profit made by the game can be added to the money made across the franchise as a whole.

> The candidate is very clear in their explanations of two reasons as to why a film company would release a video game linked to a film. First, they clearly understand the way a linked product such as a video game can assist the promotion of another product. They also clearly exemplify this by referring to the set product of *The Lego Movie*, which is important in order to fully meet the assessment criteria. In their second explanation, a different reason is given for why the release of an accompanying video game is beneficial; this time in terms of profit. The candidate also refers to the set product and, finally, they make good use of relevant terminology such as **franchise** and **synergy** when explaining their points.

Exam tip

If you are asked to refer to the set product you have studied then you must do so, using it as an example to help answer the question. For instance, in a 4–mark question – like Question 7 - the examiners would expect a detailed explanation in a single sentence for 2 marks and an appropriate example for the remaining 2 marks.

Media industries

REVISED

Background to *The Lego Movie* franchise

Lego, the Danish toy-making company established in 1949, is one of the world's leading brands. As recently as 2003, however, the company was on the verge of failing. Ventures into other markets, such as film-making, have helped Lego to climb back to the top of the toy-making world. *The Lego Movie* was Lego's first attempt to move into Hollywood and its success was a key reason behind the company's recent growth.

The Lego Movie was produced by Warner Bros, an example of a major, global film studio. Why did Lego decide to work with Warner Bros on the production of the film? Why did it then go further to work with TT Fusion on the release of *The Lego Movie* video game? These are some of the questions you will need to consider in order to successfully answer Question 7.

Tent-pole production

A **tent-pole production** is a film that conglomerates such as Warner Bros expect to make vast profits – and these profits can be used to fund other projects. The idea of a tent pole comes from the way the film can support other projects, just like a tent pole holds up the rest of the tent.

> **Tent pole production**: a film that can make large profits to support funding of other projects.

A tent-pole production may also be expected to support the sale of tie-in merchandise – products that are associated with the film.

Understanding and applying this key term will help you analyse the reasons behind Warner Bros' decision to produce *The Lego Movie*.

> **Revision activity**
>
> Go online to find examples of merchandise products related to *The Lego Movie*. Make a list of all the products you find.
>
> What kind of advertising and income-stream possibilities do these products offer Warner Bros?
>
> Continue your internet research to find the Lego film projects that have happened, or are planned, since the release of the original *Lego Movie*.
>
> Consider whether these films would have been possible without the tent-pole production's initial success?
>
> Consider what could have happened to the genre of animated, toy-based films if *The Lego Movie* had not been a success.

Synergy

Different areas of the media industry will often work together in order to promote the same product. This same idea can also be applied to the way different areas of the same company often assist one another in promotion and earning extra revenue.

The Lego Movie offers a good example of this process of **synergy**. One reason behind its success was the ensemble cast of superhero characters drawn from DC Comics. For example, the film featured Batman as one of the main characters and a whole host of Master Builders, including:

- Superman
- Wonder Woman
- Green Lantern
- Flash.

DC Comics is owned by the **conglomerate** Warner Bros. It is interesting to note the characters owned by Warner Bros didn't end at this list. Albus Dumbledore, from *Harry Potter*, and Gandalf the Wizard, from *Lord of the Rings*, are also featured in the video game. Warner Bros also owns the copyright on these creations, too.

> **Synergy**: the promotion of linked products across different areas of the media. For example, Lego released several products that helped to promote the film itself, such as Minifigures of characters in the film, and building sets.

> **Exam tip**
>
> Referring to relevant media terminology, such as **conglomerate**, will help you pick up extra marks in the exam. Be sure to use these terms regularly and accurately.

> **Revision activity**
>
> 1 Can you think of the advantages for Warner Bros of using a cast of characters they already own the copyright for?
> 2 Why would Lego, as a toy company, also be enthusiastic about this decision?
>
> **Answers on p. 135**

Regulation in the film industry

REVISED

As mentioned, the British Board of Film Classification (BBFC) regulates the film industry in the UK. Films are awarded U, PG, 12A, 15 and 18 certificates. The BBFC awards these certificates based on factors such as explicit language and themes such as sex, violence or drug use. It also has the power to make cuts to films it deems to be too explicit in order for them to be shown in the cinema or on home release.

Why was *The Lego Movie* awarded a 'U' certificate?

In addition to the short 'insight' description the BBFC provides for use on posters and advertising (in this case 'Contains mild fantasy violence and very mild language'), the BBFC provides a more detailed breakdown of content on its website. This is an extract from the BBFCinsight on the content of The Lego Movie:

> No one is seen to get hurt and the fact that all the fighting involves animated toy figures means that the fantasy nature of the violence is very clear.

The film was therefore awarded a 'U' certificate – meaning 'Universal'. This means the BBFC feels it is appropriate for any age group.

Revision activity

1 Why is it important for film regulation to exist?
2 Can you think of any reasons why some people might be against film regulation?
3 The BBFC used to be known as the British Board of Film Censors. Why do you think it changed its name?
4 Why might film-makers worry about the classification they are given? For example, why might some action films need to achieve a 15 or 18 classification?
5 Why do you think Warner Bros would have been very keen for the film to receive a 'U' certificate? (Think about the way media industries aim to target particular audiences.)

Answers on p. 135

Now have a go at this exam-style question:

Exam practice

Question 7

Explain two factors affecting the regulation of the film industry.

You may want to refer to:
● the role of the BBFC and what it does when it regulates films
● why it is important for film-makers to receive certain classifications in order to appeal to particular audiences.

[4]

Make sure you refer to the set product of *The Lego Movie* in your response.

Before you begin, take a look at the following sample response – what could be improved?

> The film industry is regulated by the BBFC and they say whether or not a film can be released. One other thing about this is that some films try to make sure they get certain age ratings so they can make more money from a particular audience.

This response succeeds in identifying what the BBFC does and the way its role can influence the way audiences are targeted. However, it does not make any mention of the set product, in this case *The Lego Movie*, which means it is a poor response overall and would only be worthy of 2 marks.

Regulation in the video game industry

REVISED

You may also be asked to respond to a question on regulation in the video game industry. The basic concept behind the way this industry is regulated is similar to that of the film industry. Many people see regulation as even more crucial when it comes to video games as they can be more easily accessed by under-age gamers who may be exposed to inappropriate content.

The Video Standards Council (VSC) uses the PEGI (Pan European Game Information) rating system to classify video games in the UK, from '3' to '7', '12', '16' and '18'. The VSC is also known as Games Rating Authority.

The Lego Movie video game was given a '7' age rating. It was important for it to receive a rating of this age to give it the widest appeal and for it to match the classification of *The Lego Movie*.

Vertical integration

REVISED

Vertical integration is an increasingly common way of operating in the media industry. This is the process whereby a single company (or merged companies) controls both the production and the supply of a product. It may be useful to think about an example of this away from the world of the media. For instance, in the chocolate industry, vertical integration could include one company owning the cocoa farm, the factories that produce and pack the chocolate and the shops the chocolate is sold in.

> **Vertical integration:** where a single company (or merged companies) controls both the production and the supply of a product.

The set products of *The Lego Movie* franchise are an excellent example of vertical integration. The developer of the *Lego Movie* video game, TT Fusion, was bought by Warner Bros in 2007 and has since produced many video games under the Lego brand. Warner Bros also owns the distribution rights to the video game and was able to release it itself. So, the supply chain can be summarised like this:

Stage of production process	Tasks involved at this stage	Company responsible
Production	Making the game: creating animations, producing soundtrack, etc.	TT Fusion – owned by Warner Bros
Distribution	Making the product available to audiences and promoting to audiences	Warner Bros

You can see from the table that Warner Bros is in control of both production and distribution of *The Lego Movie*. The same actors starring in the film reprised their roles by doing the voice acting for the video game and the game shared similar themes and narratives. This allowed Warner Bros to capitalise on the success of the film and efficiently produce a video game that was similarly profitable. Of course, both the film and video game also helped to increase profits for the Lego toy company. So all the companies involved benefited.

Exam practice

Question 7

Vertical integration is a common form of ownership in the media industry. Explain two benefits of this type of ownership for media companies.

You may want to consider the following:
● How does vertical integration help to increase profits?
● How does vertical integration make the production process more efficient?
● How does vertical integration help to increase the exposure of one brand or franchise? [4]

Cross-platform release

Platform is a term used to describe how audiences access a media product. For example, films are now available across a variety of platforms to suit the busy and varied lives of audiences, from home releases such as DVD and Blu-ray, to online streaming and digital download, to the good old-fashioned cinema. Video games are also increasingly available on a multitude of platforms – gone are the days when video games were released for one particular console.

> **Platform**: the way in which audiences can access a media product. For example, *The Lego Movie* was made available through platforms such as DVD, Blu-ray, online streaming and, of course, the cinema.

The Lego Movie video game is no exception to this. Warner Bros made the decision to release the game across various platforms, including:
● Microsoft Windows
● Nintendo 3DS
● PlayStation 3
● PlayStation 4
● PlayStation Vita
● Wii U
● Xbox 360
● Xbox One.

In addition, *The Lego Movie* video game was released on a mobile platform.

Revision activity

Many people now play games on their smartphone.
● Go online and find some facts and figures about the value of the mobile game market – how much is it worth?
● What does this suggest to you about the future of gaming?
● If you can, find some specific figures in relation to *The Lego Movie* video game.
● Look at reviews of the differences between the console and the mobile version of the game.

Read the exam practice question on page 46 again and then look at the following sample answer and the assessment comment.

> A film company would release a video game linked to a film for lots of reasons. For example, the promotion of the video game is easier if it is linked to a film. Also, more people would be likely to buy the video game if it's based on a film.

This response could only be given a maximum of 2 marks (the equivalent of a Level 2), as it shows a limited understanding of the film industry.

Now time yourself to see if you can produce a better answer in four minutes. But first consider these questions:

- What has the candidate missed out? In particular, what should they have mentioned?
- Which key terms could they have referred to?
- How fully has the candidate explained their points?

Now test yourself

TESTED

1 Write down a definition of a tent-pole film in your own words.
2 Explain why *The Lego Movie* is a good example of synergy.
3 Explain one benefit of the ensemble cast of *The Lego Movie* for different areas of the Warner Bros conglomerate.
4 Why would Warner Bros choose to release the video game on many different platforms?
5 Why is the mobile platform market so useful for contemporary audiences?

Answers on p. 133

How to prepare for the exam

- Remember that many of the decisions behind the release and promotion of *The Lego Movie* were made to create profit – this may inform the basis of many of your answers.
- Make sure you are aware of the link between media industries and how they target audiences.
- Test your knowledge of terminology you have covered by creating revision flashcards and testing yourself with friends or family.

Question 8

What this question involves

REVISED

Question 8 is a 10-mark knowledge and understanding question about film, advertising or video games. It is likely to be about media audiences but can cover any area of the theoretical framework. However, you will not be asked about media language, representation or audiences in relation to the film industry.

Timing

REVISED

Question 8 is a short essay question that should take about ten minutes.

What the examiner is looking for

REVISED

Examiners are looking for answers that show knowledge and understanding of specific areas of the theoretical framework. You will be asked only about media industries for questions about the film industry and *The Lego Movie*, while you could be asked about media language, representation or audiences for questions on the way the film was promoted. You will only be asked about media industries, audiences or intertextuality for questions on *The Lego Movie* video game.

Exam practice

Question 8

Explain at least two uses and gratifications of video games using Blumler and Katz's theory. Refer to *The Lego Movie* video game to support your answer. [10]

How to use theory

Uses and gratifications

This is one of the theories you will need to be familiar with in order to do well in your GCSE exam. Blumler and Katz were interested in the way media audiences use media products to suit their own needs and take enjoyment – or gratification – from consuming media products. Unlike previous media theories on the way audiences and media products interact, they believed that audiences are active consumers and do not make passive choices about the media they consume or enjoy.

There are four main uses and gratifications you should know about.

1 **Entertainment:**
the pleasure gained from being entertained by a media product and escaping from the 'real world' for a while.

2 **Personal identity:**
some audiences may identify with certain figures in the media, seeing them as role models and aspiring to be like them.

3 **Surveillance:**
we often use the media to gain an understanding of the world around us, e.g. watching television news will give us information on current affairs.

4 **Social interaction/social integration/personal relationships:**
we use the media to keep in touch with those around us – especially, perhaps, those who we cannot keep in contact with on a daily basis. Social media is increasingly used for this purpose.

Exam tip

Referring to relevant media theory **and** applying this to the set products will show the examiner your depth of understanding and will help to gain you higher marks.

In the exam you may be asked to think about how the Uses and Gratifications theory could apply to your study of *The Lego Movie* or *The Lego Movie* video game. Here are some ideas – can you add your own examples, too?

Use/ gratification	Example in *The Lego Movie* advertising	Example in *The Lego Movie* video game	Your own specific example from either text
Entertainment/ diversion	The narrative of the film is entertaining – we are thrust into a fantasy world and follow a 'regular' character (just like us) who takes on an extraordinary challenge – to stop the evil Lord Business. This entertaining spectacle is added to with mystery and humour throughout the film.	The video game is centred around entertainment: players take the role of characters from the film and must problem solve to construct objects as either Regular Builders (such as Emmet) or Master Builders (such as Batman) as the game progresses and becomes increasingly challenging.	

Identification	Audiences may identify with a range of characters in the film, but especially with Emmet, who represents the 'normal', everyday member of society who can make an incredible difference to the world they live in.	As with the film, players may identify with particular characters they play. Additionally, audiences might identify with the values or themes of the game – for example, the overarching concept of the battle between good and evil and the quest to defeat Lord Business.	
Social interaction/ personal relationships	Film texts can offer audiences the chance to forge and maintain personal relationships. *The Lego Movie* is no different – especially in the way the themes and content of the film could bring together young and older audiences in a shared interest for Lego.	As we have seen, *The Lego Movie* video game can be played across a variety of platforms. All of these platforms offer the ability to play as single or multiplayer – it is the multiplayer function that offers the most opportunity for social interaction. There is no option to play online against virtual opponents in the game – however, lots of audiences choose to discuss the game in online forums. How does this offer social interaction?	
Surveillance	*The Lego Movie* may offer children information about the world, such as the message that each individual can make a difference to society and the people around them.		

Read the exam practice question on page 52 again and then the sample answer and the assessment comment that follows.

Example 1

One gratification people take from playing video games is entertainment. For example, if you are bored sitting at home then you can be entertained for hours by playing a video game because they have so many levels and options to do.

Also, another gratification is that you can interact with other people by playing video games. For example, you can chat to people you play online with or you can play a video game against someone else and this lets you interact and have fun with other people.

Exam tip

If the question asks you to refer to the set product you have studied then you must do so, using it as an example to help answer the question. Failure to do this would result in a poor response.

This is a poor response and would be given around 4 marks out of 10 in the exam and would be a low Level 2. This is because it is not detailed enough and does not refer to the set product, as the question asks. If you do not refer to the set products, you will not be able to gain high marks in the exam.

Exam practice

Question 8

Explain how *The Lego Movie* promotional campaign targeted a range of audiences. [10]

Audiences are targeted in many ways by media products. The marketing and promotion of 'The Lego Movie' was specifically designed to attract and appeal to a range of audiences. For example, the poster campaign features genre conventions of a family-friendly, action adventure film, with elements of mise-en-scène such as the use of a bright colour palette and array of characters who are running away from what appears to be comic danger. This would target an audience of younger children who may already be familiar with Lego toys and video games.

However, there are also elements of the promotional campaign which target a much more mature audience. For example, the inclusion of characters such as Batman in the main theatrical poster appeals to older audiences who have grown up with comic book stories of this classic superhero. Similarly, older audiences are also targeted by the promotional character posters, such as one which features the character of Vitruvius in close up, voiced by Morgan Freeman. The actor is emphasised at the top of the poster which may help to target older audiences who are familiar with his work and lend credibility to the marketing of the film. Finally, the TV spot helps to target older audiences through the use of links to brands they may be familiar with, such as the way Premier Inn and confused.com advertise their services through the use of Lego Minifigures.

Finally, female audiences are also targeted through the promotional campaign. Wyldstyle is given a prominent role both in the foreground of the main theatrical poster and in a close up shot of her own character poster. This suggests The Lego Movie does not simply aim to appeal to a male audience who might traditionally be more associated with the toy brand, but instead is widening its appeal throughout the marketing campaign.

The candidate has done well to give a detailed response as required of a 10-mark question. They have shown they have an in-depth understanding of the entire promotional campaign. They mention the main theatrical poster, but also two different character posters and the TV ad break, with specific examples mentioned from each element of the campaign. Within these references, they have also shown an insightful understanding of the way *The Lego Movie* franchise does not target simply one audience, but looks to appeal to a range of demographics including both young and older generations and both genders. Furthermore, the candidate has referred to all the relevant media language and terminology.

All of these points combined have produced a very well written response that would be worthy of full marks.

Targeting audiences

Take a look at Figure 1.1 to see how the process of designing a promotional campaign works in the media industry.

Stage 1: Targeting	Media producers decide on the key **demographics** (categories) of audiences they want to target. For example, they may base this on demographics such as age, gender, ethnicity.

Stage 2: Deciding strategy	Media producers decide on their promotional strategy in order to target the audience they have identified. They then create test products and gain audience feedback on whether a small focus group of the target audience feels the promotional campaign may be effective.

Stage 3: Campaign launch	Media producers use the feedback they have been given to make any changes and then launch their advertising campaign. This may take the form of promotion through strategies such as television advertising, print media products such as posters and billboards, online advertising or social media campaigns.

Figure 1.1 The steps involved in designing a promotional campaign

Now test yourself

1 Write down as many examples of audience demographics as you can think of.
2 Why is it important for media producers to gain audience feedback before a promotional campaign is launched?
3 Why would it be important for the best promotional campaigns to use more than just one form of promotion? What would be the result of targeting different audiences across a variety of promotional platforms?

Answers on p. 133

You have been asked to study both the print advertising campaign and the film trailer which appeared on TV. Let's take a look at the print adverts first and see how they have been constructed to target audiences. You can find the main theatrical release poster here: http://www.impawards.com/2014/lego_movie_ver9.html

Conventions refer to the key features of a media product. The conventions of film posters include:

- film title
- central image
- tagline
- release date
- actors' names (not shown in this poster)
- credit block (the small text at the bottom of the poster showing actors names and production company information).

Conventions: the key features of a media product.

The first four of these conventions all help to create meaning and target audiences in this poster.

The title of the film is prominently placed in the upper third of the poster. Its design is made of the traditional Lego bricks which would immediately appeal to fans of the toy brand. The words of the title are also suspended from a crane which has suggestions of being 'under construction'. This would also help to target audiences of fans of Lego as the object of using the bricks is to build and construct projects.

Second, mise-en-scène is also crucial in targeting the demographic audience of young children. The central image which shows the ensemble cast of characters uses a bright colour palette which would attract a young audience. Furthermore, the main protagonist Emmet is instantly recognisable through his yellow face which is symbolic of Lego Minifigures and again would appeal to an audience of Lego fans. His facial expression is one of panic, which suggests the film will follow an action-packed storyline, especially as the rest of the characters are also running away from danger.

Exam tip

Remember to look at aspects such as the release date, which is an important part of any film poster. The half-term holiday, for example, is vital for a film aimed at a family audience.

Revision activity

Using the example above, think about how you could analyse the use of both the tagline and design of the release date in the same way. Think about the following:
- what the tagline suggests the film might be about and how it could appeal to an audience
- the purpose of the release date and the meaning of the word 'assembling'.
Write up your answers in two short paragraphs.

The print advertising campaign also featured close-up shots of some of the main cast members such as Wyldstyle or Vitruvius. You can find the character poster of Wyldstyle here: http://www.impawards.com/2014/lego_movie_ver7.html

You can find the character poster of Vitruvius here: http://www.impawards.com/2014/lego_movie_ver3.html

Other posters you may use to respond to an exam question feature Emmet and Lord Business in similar framing.

Revision activity

After looking at all the posters closely, think about the following:
- Why do you think the producers of the posters decided to use close-up shots?
- What is suggested about Wyldstyle's character through her name and elements of mise-en-scène such as her hair, make-up and clothing?
- What demographic would the poster of Wyldstyle help to attract? Why could it be important for Warner Bros to target this audience?
- On the poster featuring Vitruvius, why is Morgan Freeman's name shown prominently? What audience demographic might this help to target?

Television promotion

Warner Bros did not advertise *The Lego Movie* just through film posters. As with all effective promotional campaigns, the company used other platforms to raise awareness about the release of the film.

One very effective form of promotion was the decision to create an entire TV 'spot', devoted to using Lego to advertise other brands. The result was a three-and-a-half-minute advert break, comprising individual adverts for British Heart Foundation, Confused.com, BT and Premier Inn. The final part of the ad break was used to promote *The Lego Movie* itself by including a small teaser trailer.

You may be asked to respond to a question that requires you to show your knowledge and understanding of the campaign by analysing the ad break. You can find the ad break on YouTube by accessing the following link: www.youtube.com/watch?v=HSbYBzUEQlc

Let's begin with the final part of the advert break, starting at 2:40. The production logos of Warner Bros (the producer and distributor) and Village Roadshow Pictures (a company also involved in the production of the film) are shown at the start of the trailer. If you look closely you will notice that they have been made out of Lego. Why was this decision made? What sort of tone does it set for the film? Why would Warner Bros want its logo to be seen before the trailer is played?

How to use theory

Narrative in the trailer

Tzvetan Todorov's narrative theory is a useful tool for analysing the narrative structure of the *Lego Movie* teaser trailer.

Fill in the rest of the table for the teaser trailer and then answer the questions that follow.

Narrative stage	Definition	How is this shown in the trailer?
Equilibrium	The 'normality'. We see characters in their normal, day-to-day life.	Emmet is shown on the sofa watching television.
Disruption	An event occurs to break the normality.	President Business makes an announcement that 'you will be put to sleep'.
Recognition of disruption	Characters realise something has gone wrong.	
Attempt to repair	Characters try to solve the problem.	
Return to equilibrium/new equilibrium	The problem is solved and things return to normal or a new equilibrium is established.	Why is this stage of the narrative not shown in a film trailer?

You will notice that the stages of equilibrium and disruption happen very quickly in the trailer, within ten seconds. The rest of the trailer then aims to give hints about what might happen in the rest of the film and introduces some other key characters.

- Given the length of the trailer, why do the equilibrium and disruption need to be shown so quickly?
- If the target audience is younger people, why does it make sense to very quickly establish the disruption in the narrative?

Exam tip

Remember, in your responses you should be carefully considering how the target audience will respond to the set products **and** the way audiences may respond *differently* to the set products.

Media language in the trailer

Revision activity

Any answer that refers to relevant media language will really help to show the examiner you know the set product well and demonstrate knowledge and understanding. Use the table and the key terms below to help you analyse the media language in the trailer and respond to the prompts under each section.

Media language element	Question 1	Question 2	Question 3
Cinematography	Several close-up shots of key characters have been used. Why?	We also see establishing shots of various locations, such as the crash on the railway bridge. What effect does this create?	The final scene shows a low-angle shot of Vitruvius and Wyldstyle. Why has this been used?
Sound	How is **diegetic** dialogue used to convey a sense of narrative?	What impact do diegetic sounds such as explosions and gunshots have?	How is **non-diegetic** sound such as background music used to create atmosphere?
Editing	Think about the pace of the trailer and look at the length of the time between cuts. What impact does this have?	Look at the **intertitles** such as 'The top treat for half term'. What kind of audience does this appeal to?	Slow motion is used at various points in the trailer. Why? What effect does this create?
Mise-en-scène	How do the various locations shown help to convey a sense of **genre**?	How would you describe the **colour palette** of the trailer? How might this help to target an audience?	What can we tell about the various characters from their costume?

Diegetic: sound within 'the world of the film'. Refers to sound that the characters and audience can hear.

Non-diegetic: sound only the audience can hear, e.g. background music.

Intertitle: the text used between shots in a trailer. Often, these are used to help explain the narrative or to show positive reviews of the film.

Genre: category of film, e.g. action adventure, fantasy, horror.

Colour palette: the range of colours used in a media text. The colours are usually kept consistent within one text.

Exam tip

In your analysis, remember some areas of media language might not be as relevant as others and there may naturally be more to say about two or three of them. But always cover them all in your response.

Revision activity

Once you have analysed the trailer using the table and prompts, try applying the same analysis techniques to the rest of the TV ad break, looking at the way the other brands have been advertised.

Targeting audiences through the *Lego Movie* ad break

Warner Bros UK worked with other media companies to produce the all-Lego ad break on early prime-time Sunday-night ITV (6 million viewers). This meant that Warners and the other companies helped one another reach a range of audiences. The ad break was so unusual that it trended on social media and was viewed over a million times in a week on YouTube, gaining extra publicity.

Revision activity

1 British Heart Foundation, Confused.com, BT and Premier Inn all paid for the production costs of their adverts themselves. What does this tell you about their desire to work with the *Lego Movie* brand?

2 Each advert is made exclusively of Lego bricks. This helps to build the 'world' made entirely of Lego. How does this theme link to *The Lego Movie*? Do you think this was a conscious decision by the marketing team behind the film?

3 Each advert is followed by a character from *The Lego Movie* such as Batman or Vitruvius. Why is this important to maintain the brand identity of the film? How does it help to remind the audience of the underlying promotional message?

4 The adverts all have a friendly, warm and humorous tone to them. Why is this important when you consider the audience *The Lego Movie* is trying to target?

5 The ad break features voiceovers from familiar names such as Vinny Jones and Lenny Henry. How might this appeal to audiences?

6 According to YouGov, which measures audience data, more than 6 million people saw the ad break. Why is this positive for both *The Lego Movie* and the featured brands?

7 How do you think audiences would respond to this ad break? Do you think they would be attracted to the campaign and be encouraged to go and see the film? Or might they see through the family-friendly characters and take a more cynical (or suspicious) view that Warner Bros is creating this product just to make money? What is your opinion?

Answers on p. 135

Exam practice

Question 8

How are audiences targeted by media products? You should refer to the set product of the promotion of *The Lego Movie* in your answer.

[10]

Important note: We have now looked at Questions 7 and 8 in this section of the exam from two main perspectives: considering issues related to media industries in Question 7 and audience-focused concepts for Question 8.

It is very important to note that, in the exam, you will not necessarily be asked to respond to each question in relation to these areas of the theoretical framework. For example, you could be asked about audience for Question 7 and media industries for Question 8, or perhaps a combination of both. You may even be given a question that tests your knowledge of

Exam tip

Remember, as long as you have revised the set products and how to apply the theoretical framework to them, you will be well prepared to answer any question that comes up.

media language or representations (which we will look at next). However, as long as you can apply the general concepts we have been discussing, you will be well prepared to answer any question that comes up.

How to prepare for the exam

- Ensure you are clear on audience theory such as Uses and Gratifications and how this links to the promotional campaign.
- Practise your understanding of media language by analysing the various elements across the entire promotional campaign.
- Aim to answer the exam-style questions and have a go at setting some of your own

Question 9

What this question involves

REVISED

This is a 10-mark question that will test your ability to analyse the set products in relation to media language and/or media representation. You may also be asked to discuss the set products in relation to their contexts.

Timing

REVISED

Question 9 is a short essay question that should take about ten minutes.

What the examiner is looking for

REVISED

The examiner is looking for your ability to analyse the set media products in relation to the area(s) of the theoretical framework you are asked about. You will not be asked to respond to a question on media language in relation to *The Lego Movie* itself – only the promotional products surrounding it.

For this question you will revise:
- *The Lego Movie* ad break including UK film trailer
- *The Lego Movie* print advertising campaign
- *The Lego Movie* video game
- media language
- representation
- your analytical skills of all areas of the theoretical framework and how they can be applied to *The Lego Movie* franchise.

Media language

Relevant elements of media language include the following:
- **genre**
- narrative
- **cinematography**
- editing
- sound
- mise-en-scène.

You will remember we have already looked at some of these aspects of media language when revising previous questions. For example, when looking at media audiences we analysed the use of cinematography, mise-en-scène and narrative structure in the trailer for *The Lego Movie* during its promotional ad break.

Genre: category of film, e.g. action adventure, fantasy, horror.

Cinematography: describes the angles and movement of the camera.

Genre

When considering genre, we need to think about the following key terms.

- Genre codes and conventions: the typical features that symbolise a genre. For example, one convention of a sci-fi film is that it is set in outer space.
- Hybrid: when a film mixes elements of different genres.
- Iconography: the visual elements, such as props, that help to symbolise a particular genre. For example, iconography of a Western film may include cowboy hats, horses and guns.
- Intertextuality: when the meaning of one media text arises from its relationship with another. For example, we understand Batman's character in *The Lego Movie* because we have seen him appear before in many other films and media products.

Revision activity

Answer the remaining questions in the table below to help you revise how these elements of genre apply to *The Lego Movie* franchise. Make a note of your answers on separate paper.

Element of genre	The poster campaign	The TV ad break	*The Lego Movie* video game
Codes and conventions	What visual elements are used to convey genre conventions? *Visual elements of mise-en-scène such as facial expressions and body language of characters suggest panic as they run from danger. This conveys the action-adventure genre.*	There is a clear difference between heroic protagonists and villainous antagonists – how does this relate to genre?	What activities/tasks can you complete in the game? What genre of game do these activities represent?
Hybridity	How does the film poster combine different film genres? *President Business's facial expression on his close-up poster suggests he is a villainous character, which is a convention of the action-adventure genre. In contrast, some characters on the main poster convey elements of the comedy genre, such as Unikitty – as we laugh at her seemingly out of place amongst a group of 'heroes'. This reflects genre hybridity.*	How does the ad break show the mixing of film genres?	How does the video game mix elements of genre? *Tasks range from puzzle levels to complete by building projects to driving missions. This shows the way the game combines different genres – taking elements from puzzle/platformers to a more high-octane, thrilling driving game.*
Iconography	What visual elements can you see that you would associate with the action-adventure genre across the poster campaign? *Props such as weaponry are examples of iconography of the action-adventure genre, as they symbolise conflict and danger, which the action-adventure genre is built around.*	What visual elements can you see that you would associate with the action-adventure genre? Or any other genre? Think about media language elements such as sound, editing and mise-en-scène.	Make a list of all the props that could be seen as examples of iconography of action-adventure.

Exam practice

Question 9

Analyse how genre codes have been used in *The Lego Movie* poster campaign to appeal to a family audience. In your answer you must refer to relevant media contexts.   [10]

Example 1

One way in which the poster campaign appeals to a family audience is in the genre codes and conventions that are shown. For example, on the main theatrical poster, the location of the large urban setting is instantly recognisable and the threat of destruction, signified by the explosions and character running from danger, conveys a family-friendly action-adventure film that will appeal to a wide range of ages.

Second, the main theatrical poster shows genre hybridity by mixing both action-adventure and superhero genres. This can be seen by the inclusion of superhero characters such as Batman, Superman and Green Lantern with the iconography of action-adventure films such as weaponry and explosions. The way the poster mixes genres suggests there is something for all audiences to enjoy and shows it is appealing to a family audience.

This answer is a strong response because it uses specific examples from the set product and terminology to answer the question well. However, it does not include any relevant media context, which can be important when answering Question 9. Look at how this could be done, as in the example below.

Example 2

The way the poster campaign has been designed to appeal to a family audience is linked to the context in which it was made. Media industries are now globalised, meaning they can reach audiences across the globe. In order to instantly appeal to these audiences, media texts must use clearly recognisable genre codes and conventions which the audience are able to identify with quickly. This, in turn, helps conglomerates like Warner Bros to draw in audiences and generate profit at the box office.

This example provides context to the way a family audience has been targeted in the promotion of *The Lego Movie*. You may also want to consider the following relevant contexts:

Context	Explanation	How does this apply to *The Lego Movie* franchise?
Feminism and **changing gender roles**	Historically, men and women have never quite held equal roles in society. We have often lived in a patriarchal world, where men dominate. However, since the 1960s we have gradually progressed to an increasingly equal society. For example, women are now expected and encouraged to pursue careers instead of raising a family at home. Feminist ideals of gender equality continue to be pursued in modern society. This includes equality between those who do not identify as either male or female, such as transsexual people.	Think about the character of Wyldstyle and her role within the game.
Reasons behind genre hybridity	What is the reason behind genre hybridity? Well, one reason is that it keeps audiences interested and entertained. By mixing genres, increasingly original ideas can be produced. As we have seen before, another answer lies in profits. Films appeal to a far wider audience by mixing genres and characters in one film and this demonstrates the context of the continual striving for profit in the film industry.	Why would Warner Bros want to include Batman and Superman (and a host of other characters) in the same film?

Now that you have an understanding of how media contexts can apply to *The Lego Movie* franchise, try to continue the exam practice question on your own. Use the previous exemplar paragraphs to help you. You might want to include:

- a further point on the way genre codes appeal to a family audience — such as the way the individual character posters combine to appeal to a wide range of family members
- a link to another relevant media context, such as the way Wyldstyle's prominent inclusion in the poster campaign could link to a post-feminist context.

Feminism: the belief in equality between genders.

Changing gender roles: the increasing role of women in public life (e.g. politics) following the impact of 1970s feminism.

Representation

REVISED

The final area we need to explore in this section is **representation**, a key concept you will be exploring throughout your course. Representation refers to the way people, groups or people or issues are portrayed in the media and the way this can shape our understanding of the world as a result.

For example, ethnicity is an issue that is often portrayed in the media. One instance of this is the way in which news media outlets have been accused of representing Muslim people as being involved in terrorism, when in fact terrorist activities throughout the world are carried out by people from all sorts of ethnic backgrounds. The representation of Muslims, however, feeds the **stereotype** of the Islamic religion often being responsible for terrorist acts.

Representation: how people, groups of people or issues are portrayed in the media and the way this can shape our understanding of the world as a result.

Stereotype: a widely held but oversimplified idea about a particular type of person or issue.

How can we think about representation in relation to *The Lego Movie* franchise?

There are various issues that are represented in the franchise. These include:

- gender
- ethnicity
- age.

Let's begin by taking a look at gender. In order to do this, we will analyse the characters of Emmet and Wyldstyle. We need to understand the key terms in relation to stereotyping and representations of gender.

Emmet is the main male protagonist of the franchise. The film and video game revolve around his transition from a normal, everyday guy to the hero that saves the world. Remember, this is exemplified by the film's tagline, 'The story of a nobody who saved everybody'. How does this portray the male gender? Well, as both products centre on a man as the main character, and he becomes the hero of the day, we could say the franchise **supports the stereotype** of men being the dominant gender.

However, if you look further into the way the franchise is promoted, there are elements of the campaign that **subvert the stereotypical representation** of men in the media. For example, in the main theatrical poster, Emmet is in the very centre of the image but his facial expression shows him running away from the danger, terrified about the situation he is in. In another example, during the TV ad break we hear Emmet scream, 'I want to go home!' while in a high-speed chase. How does this help to challenge the stereotypical representations of gender we often see in the media?

Exam tip

Always be on the lookout for evidence of stereotyping or instances of when a media text challenges stereotypical roles. These make useful points for analysis.

Support stereotypical representations: reinforce the typical portrayal of a person or issue in the media.

Subvert stereotypical representations: challenge or go against the typical portrayal of a person or issue in the media.

Revision activity

Look closely at the TV ad break. How does Emmet respond to Wyldstyle's claim of 'We would rather he died'? You may also want to look at the trailer for *The Lego Movie* video game. Does Emmet seem in control? How is he portrayed? Does his representation support or subvert stereotypes? Or does it do both?

Wyldstyle herself offers another interesting portrayal of gender. Look again at the representation of Wyldstyle in her character poster and in the main theatrical poster. Then consider the following points:

- the elements of her portrayal that support stereotypical representations of females
- the elements of her portrayal that subvert stereotypical representations of females
- the role that Wyldstyle plays in bringing in a wider audience.

This last point leads to the question of context which, remember, is vital when answering Question 9. Wyldstyle links to the post-feminist context of the franchise, as she is represented as a strong, independent character who is equal, if not superior, in ability to the male characters in both the film and the video game. This is supported in the film's poster campaign as she is given a prominent role in both the main theatrical poster and the character poster.

One final character we can analyse in relation to interesting points on representation is Vitruvius. Named after the Ancient Roman engineer, he is a wise and noble wizard who teaches Emmet that the key to true

Revision activity

Look again at the TV ad break for *The Lego Movie* and the trailer for *The Lego Movie* video game. Wyldstyle is featured heavily. What can you hear her say? What do you see her do? How do these aspects contribute to her representation and the wider portrayal of females in general?

building is to listen to yourself and follow the instructions in your head. In comparison to Emmet and Wyldstyle, who appear in classic Lego yellow, Vitruvius's skin is dark and he is clearly an old man. This raises the following points:

- Vitruvius subverts a media stereotype of ethnic minorities often being seen as 'troublesome' or associated with negative actions such as crime
- Vitruvius challenges another media stereotype of the older generation as grumpy and not being as able as they once were (in Pixar's animated adventure *Up*, Vitruvius also challenges this).

To help you bring together your thoughts on representation in the franchise, copy out the following table and record your ideas.

Revision activity

Representational issue	Relevant character	Supports or subverts stereotypes?	Evidence from the set products (film posters or video game)
Gender (men)			
Gender (females)			
Ethnicity			
Age			

Exam practice

Question 9

Analyse representations of gender in *The Lego Movie* poster campaign. [10]

Take a look at the following sample answer.

Example 1

Gender is portrayed in some unusual ways in the poster campaign for The Lego Movie. For example, in the main theatrical poster, we see two examples of female characters: Wyldstyle and Wonder Woman. Mise-en-scène suggests both characters subvert stereotypical representations of gender, as Wyldstyle is shown with a fierce facial expression, suggesting she is ready for combat which challenges typical portrayals of femininity. Similarly, Wonder Woman is shown with the prop of a lasso, showing her ability to carry out violent acts, which also subverts our stereotypical expectations of gender.

See if you can add to this exemplar response by looking at other aspects of representation of gender. Ensure you refer to specific examples and aim to analyse:

- representation of men
- the extent to which stereotypes of gender are reinforced or subverted
- the rest of the poster campaign, such as the character posters.

Compare your response with Example 2:

Example 2

In some instances, men are portrayed in a stereotypical fashion in the promotional campaign. For example, the character poster of Lord Business clearly portrays him as the evil protagonist, through elements of mise-en-scène such as his furious facial expression and intimidating costume. This may suggest connotations of a stereotypically masculine antagonist. His physical dominance over the other characters is also emphasised in the main theatrical poster, where he towers over the rest of the cast and they are running away from the danger seemingly caused by him.

However, men are also portrayed in ways which could suggest stereotypes are subverted. For example, the character poster of Emmet shows a close-up of his face in sheer panic. This challenges the way men have often been cast as the heroes of adventure films, with their role to be stereotypically manly and 'save the day'. This representation is emphasised in the main theatrical poster as Emmet is shown leading the crowd running from danger, but unlike the other characters he seems to be the only one who is afraid, connoted by his terrified facial expression which is in a stark contrast to the concentrated expression of the other characters.

The way The Lego Movie franchise challenges stereotypical representations of gender could link to the context in which the film is made. We are now entering an era in which media products reflect a post-feminist society – one in which there is more equality between genders – and increasingly films and video games reflect the way people no longer feel the need to conform to strict boundaries surrounding identities of gender.

First, this is a detailed response, which is required of a 10-mark question as you are expected to write in more depth than say for Question 7. Second, the candidate has shown they have the insight and understanding to recognise the various representations in the campaign and the way these either reinforce or subvert stereotypes.

These points are supported by specific examples from across the poster material, which demonstrates a greater understanding. Finally, the candidate manages to link these representations to the overall context in which the franchise was produced and this really helps to lend a sophistication and maturity to their response, which would be worthy of a very strong response to this question

Now test yourself

TESTED

1 What do we mean by genre hybridity?
2 Give two examples of iconography from the action-adventure genre.
3 What is a stereotype?
4 If someone classes themselves as a feminist, what do they believe in?
5 How does the character of Vitruvius challenge stereotypes of age?

Answers on p. 133

How to prepare for the exam

- Revise the specific genre conventions of *The Lego Movie* and how these are shown in the promotional material and video game.
- Ensure you are familiar with the relevant areas of representation – gender, age and ethnicity - and how these are portrayed across the promotional campaign.
- Practise the sample questions in this section to get used to extended essay writing. If you can, try to create your own exam-style questions to answer based on the content you have revised.

▶ Paper 2 – Section A: Music

What you have to do

This section of the exam asks five questions on your study of music across three media forms:
- an in-depth study of magazines, with *Mojo* magazine as the set product
- a study of music videos, with two music videos as the set product
- a study of radio, with BBC Radio 1 *Live Lounge* as the set product.

Which areas of the theoretical framework must I study?	
Music magazines	The whole theoretical framework: ● media language ● media representations ● media industries ● media audiences plus social/cultural contexts
Music videos	● media language ● media representations ● a small part of media audiences plus social/cultural contexts
Music radio	● media industries ● media audiences plus social/cultural and political contexts

The five questions will be as follows:

Q1	1 mark	This question will ask for knowledge and you should write a very short answer.
Q2	4 marks	This question will ask for knowledge and understanding, so your answer should be at least two sentences, taking about four minutes to answer.
Q3	10 marks	This question will ask for knowledge and understanding, so your answer should be a short essay, taking about ten minutes to answer.
Q4	5 marks	This question will ask you to analyse either an extract given in the exam or one set product (magazine or video) in terms of media language or representation, taking about five minutes to answer. It may ask you to refer to contexts.
Q5	15 marks	This question will ask you to analyse extracts from two magazines in the exam paper in terms of media language or representation and come to a judgement and conclusion about them. This longer essay should take about 15 minutes to answer. It may ask you to refer to contexts.

Question 1

What this question involves

This is a 1-mark knowledge-only question about radio, magazines or music video. It is likely to focus on media industries and audiences, but could cover any area of the theoretical framework.

Timing

This is a short question that should take less than one minute.

What the examiner is looking for

Examiners are looking for correct answers. The answer might be something such as a definition of a key term, a fact about the media industries, or the name of a regulator.

Factual questions are likely to be about media industries, but any area could come up in this question. For media industries, you should revise facts about regulation and ownership (for magazines and radio only) and the meaning of key terms.

Media industries facts for magazines and radio

Industry	Media regulator
Magazines	Independent Press Standards Organisation (IPSO) or Impress (*Mojo* has joined IPSO)
Radio	Ofcom

Media owners for set products	
Mojo	Bauer Media
Radio 1	BBC, a public corporation established by a Royal Charter

Now test yourself

1 Identify the owner of *Mojo* magazine.
2 Identify the regulator for radio.
3 The owner of *Mojo* magazine also owns radio stations. Identify the term for branching out into other areas of business.
4 Bauer Media owns magazines and radio stations. Identify the term used to describe such a company.

Answers on p. 133

How to prepare for the exam

- Create a glossary of all the key terms you use as part of the course, with a definition of each one. Learn any media industries and audiences key terms.
- Memorise the regulators for magazines and radio.
- Learn the names of the owners of each of the set products you have studied:
  - Radio 1 (the BBC, a public corporation)
  - *Mojo* magazine (Bauer Media).

Questions 2 and 3

What these questions involve

REVISED

Question 2 is a 4-mark knowledge and understanding question about radio, magazines or music video, so can cover any area of the theoretical framework, including media industries and audiences.

Question 3 is a 10-mark knowledge and understanding question about radio, magazines or music video, so can cover any area of the theoretical framework, including media industries and audiences.

Timing

REVISED

Question 2 is a short question that should take about four minutes.

Question 3 is a short essay question that should take about ten minutes.

What the examiner is looking for

REVISED

The examiner is looking for answers that show knowledge and understanding of specific areas of the theoretical framework – media language, representations, industries or audiences – applied to music magazines, music videos and/or radio.

If the question asks you to refer to the set product you have studied then you must do so, using it as an example to help answer the question. Question 2 might ask you for one explanation and one example for the 4 marks – the examiner would then be looking for a detailed explanation (though only one sentence) for 2 marks and an appropriate example for the second 2 marks. Question 3 might be a short essay question requiring you to refer to the set product. Again, the examiner would be looking for the ability to both answer the question and use the set product as an example. If you didn't use the set product, this would suggest a poor grade essay.

Exam practice

Question 2
Explain one way that music videos use media language to differ from one another. Refer to one example of contrasting language in two music videos you have studied to support your answer. [4]

In this question, examiners are looking for an explanation of one way in which one of the following elements of media language is used differently in music videos, perhaps to fit different artists or different musical genres:
● camerawork
● editing
● mise-en-scène
● narrative.

For the example to be relevant, you will need to pick an element that is different in the two music videos you have studied and explain clearly how it contrasts in the two videos.

Read the following sample answers and the assessment comments after them.

Example 1

Music videos look very different to one another. They use different narrative. Beyoncé tells a story about men behaving badly. Mark Ronson tells a story about men dancing.

This answer would be awarded 2 marks: 1 mark for identifying narrative as a difference in use of media language (this is not explained enough for 2 marks) and 1 mark for describing the narrative of the two videos – but only 1 mark because it is not clearly established how they are different.

Example 2

Music videos often use mise-en-scène differently in music videos to create connotations that fit the artist and the song. They might choose different settings, costumes, lighting and performance. For example, the Wheatus video uses a suburban high-school setting, costumes that would be worn by mainstream teenagers, and acting that makes the main character look shy and lacking in confidence. The Avril Lavigne video, by contrast, uses an urban setting, costumes reflecting a 'biker' subculture, and performance that makes the main character look confident and in control.

Exam tip

This question does not specify which music video you have to use, as you have a choice of music videos to study.

This answer would achieve 4 marks. It offers an explanation of how music videos can use different media language, for the first 2 marks, and goes on to give examples of contrasting media language use in two videos – using the mise-en-scène for both videos, which helps create the contrast, earning the second 2 marks.

Exam practice

Question 3

Explain how and why producers of radio programmes target different audiences. Refer to the Radio 1 *Live Lounge* to support your answer.

[10]

This question specifies which radio programme you have to use, as you have no choice over the one set product you study. Examiners are looking for two explanations:
● how producers target different audiences
● why producers target different audiences.
They are looking for good use of the Radio 1 *Live Lounge* to illustrate this. You could compare the audience targeting of this programme to programmes on a very different radio station, for example Classic FM. As this is a question focusing on the media form, it is fine also to use other radio stations as long as you refer to the set product.

For these questions you will revise:
● all the relevant areas of the theoretical framework for the three media forms as these could come up, but Questions 2 and 3 are more likely to be about radio and music videos.

Media form	What you should revise
Radio	Industries and audience
Music videos	Media language, representations, how audiences gain a sense of identity from music videos and might interpret them differently
Magazines	The whole framework, but industries and audience are more likely for Questions 2 and 3; media language and representations will be covered under Questions 4 and 5

Radio industries and audiences

REVISED

Commercial radio

Radio producers are both commercial and publicly owned. Commercial stations include national, regional and local stations. Bauer Media, the publisher of *Mojo* magazine, for example, runs national stations such as Classic Rock, Kiss FM and Absolute Radio as well as online-only and local stations. This **diversification** into radio as well as publishing makes Bauer Media a media **conglomerate**. Commercial stations target different audiences to:

- attract advertisers interested in a **niche market** (e.g. a specialised audience such as young people or local people)
- find a new audience by filling an otherwise unfilled niche in the market (e.g. a radio station launched in 2017 aimed at builders)
- attract a **mass audience** to bring in mass advertising.

BBC radio

The BBC has delivered radio since the 1920s as part of **Public Service Broadcasting (PSB)**. The initial role of the BBC was to raise the cultural standards of the nation, so it resisted playing solely popular music until 1967, when Radio 1 was born – before then, popular music was always mixed with music considered to be more culturally significant, e.g. classical music.

The social/cultural context

Commercially successful music, such as mainstream pop music, is considered to be less important by media producers than music aimed at a specialised audience. Classical music is considered to be more artistic than pop music, but so is jazz – a more modern form.

Live performance is regarded as more culturally significant than simply playing records. It is also much more expensive. Radio 3, for example, is given a large enough budget to broadcast live classical music performances. The BBC can both afford to do this and needs to do so to fit its PSB requirements.

The political context

There have been political debates about whether Radio 1 should be seen as PSB broadcasting. This is because political decision-makers share the belief that mainstream popular music is not culturally important, so playing popular music is not seen as informing or educating audiences. Some politicians called for Radio 1 to be sold to the commercial sector and be funded by advertising. They argue that it is not really different to commercial pop music radio, so shouldn't be funded by the public. The BBC has responded to these criticisms by:

Diversification: when institutions branch out into other industries to limit risk.

Conglomerate: a large (often multinational) business organisation, which owns a number of different companies; a media conglomerate owns businesses in different media forms.

Niche market: media users with a special interest or of a specific demographic.

Mass audience: large number of media users.

Public Service Broadcasting (PSB): broadcasting that has to follow particular Ofcom requirements and, in the case of the BBC, follow its Reithian traditions.

- making Radio 1 more appealing to younger listeners – which fitted the requirement to cater for all audiences and **reflect the diversity** of the country across its stable of stations
- reducing the age of the Radio 1 audience by deliberately not appealing to older audiences, which makes the station different from commercial mass market stations
- introducing programmes such as *Live Lounge* that bring distinctively PSB content in offering live performance.

> **Reflect diversity**: an inclusive approach that caters for all the varied cultural groups in our society.

BBC radio audiences

Radio 1 is part of a stable of radio stations designed to cover a range of tastes and cater for every audience.

	Targets
Radio 1	15–29 year olds with popular music
Radio 1Xtra	Fans of black music
Radio 2	A mass audience with a mix of speech and music
Radio 3	Fans of high culture with classical music, arts programmes and drama
Radio 4	An educated mass audience with news, current affairs, comedy, drama and documentaries
Radio 5 Live	News and sports fans
BBC 6 Music	The discerning popular music fan by including rarities and older music
BBC Asian network	British Asians

> **Exam tip**
>
> You do not need to memorise this list of stations, but you should understand that Radio 1 is part of a larger whole.

The BBC aims to fulfil its PSB requirement to reflect diversity and serve all audiences with **distinctive** programming across this range of stations. These requirements are only partly due to regulation by Ofcom. More importantly, the BBC has to justify charging the licence fee to every household with a television, so it needs to serve all audiences.

> **Distinctive**: in the context of PSB, having specific characteristics that make the channel different from other channels, especially commercial channels.

Convergence

The Radio 1 *Live Lounge* is a good example of **convergence**. The sessions are:

- played on the radio
- broadcast on BBC Four television
- available as CDs
- available online via the BBC iPlayer or the BBC Radio 1 channel on YouTube.

YouTube is now the most used means of accessing popular music among British audiences, so the BBC's presence is crucial to its continuing success. It is also accessed by an international audience, fitting the BBC's remit to represent Britain to the world.

> **Convergence**: the merging of previously separate media forms in one entity; for example, we use smartphones to stream music.

How to use theory

Uses and Gratifications

The audience may use radio for a range of uses and gratifications.

Personal identity

Clearly targeted radio stations may offer a sense of personal identity to audiences. Among the BBC stations:
- listening to Radio 1 may offer a sense of a youthful identity
- Radio 3 gives the sense of a cultured identity
- BBC Asian network brings the sense of a British Asian identity
- local radio stations may offer local identity
- the Radio 1 *Live Lounge* may offer a sense of being a fan of authentic live performance, in opposition to the manufactured nature of recorded music.

Social interaction and integration

- Radio is often used as a background to other activities in the home, in the car or at work. This can offer a sense of companionship to people in isolated settings, e.g. the housebound.

- News and current affairs programming can offer a sense of being British, or being local.
- Audiences can interact with their favourite radio programmes by calling in, texting or on social media.
- The Radio 1 *Live Lounge* may offer opportunities for Twitter conversation due to its unusual content – bands playing other bands' songs.

Entertainment

Radio offers a full range of entertainment – nearly every television genre or format was invented by radio. The Radio 1 *Live Lounge*, for example, offers the predictability of a regular format and presenter with the originality of each performance, and the added unpredictability of live radio.

Surveillance

- Radio offers a sense of being in contact with the world.
- It gives information about the world of popular music or the wider world through news, current affairs and documentaries.
- The Radio 1 *Live Lounge* offers further insight into the musical abilities of the featured artists.

Read the Exam practice Question 3 on page 71 again. Then answer the question yourself in ten minutes.

Now look at the following full sample answer.

> Producers of radio programmes may work for commercial radio or publicly owned radio. Commercial radio stations such as Kiss FM have to find an audience they can sell to advertisers. They do this by choosing particular genres and eras of music to play, by advertising and marketing their brand, and by choosing presenters that fit this brand. Pop music stations like Kiss FM can reach young audiences that are hard for advertisers to reach, so are valuable. Some stations like Classic FM attract a more upmarket audience that advertisers will also pay money to reach. Commercial stations will target different audiences to find a niche in the market that hasn't been met, e.g. a radio station aimed at builders, to attract mass audiences to sell to mass brand advertisers, e.g. Capital Radio, or to attract a niche market that is valuable to advertisers, e.g. Classic FM.
>
> BBC radio stations don't have to attract advertisers, but they do have to fulfil the BBC's Public Service Broadcasting requirements. These include reflecting the diversity of Britain, serving all audiences, and producing distinctive radio programmes. The BBC does this by offering a stable of radio channels that between them serve diverse audiences by offering different genres of music and different presentational styles. Radio 1Xtra and the BBC Asian network target black and Asian listeners. BBC local radio targets local audiences all around

the country. Radio 2 targets an older mass audience who like pop music. Radio 3 targets a niche target audience who like classical music. This is a good example of distinctive radio, as Radio 3 will play difficult classical music – especially modern music – that targets a very niche audience, which commercial stations such as Classic FM would avoid.

The Radio 1 Live Lounge fits into this by targeting young audiences: 15-29 year olds. The Live Lounge attracts audiences who like the authenticity of live music. Targeting this audience rather than fans of mainstream pop music fits the PSB requirement to be distinctive – live music is considered 'superior' to recorded music as it requires musicianship and is more expensive to produce, so won't be found on commercial radio. Choosing a young black woman to present the Live Lounge fits this audience targeting as well as helping the BBC reflect the diversity of the British audience.

This answer fits the Level 3 mark band (7–10 marks) because it explains both 'how' and 'why' radio producers target audiences with reference to the Radio 1 *Live Lounge* in terms of target audience. It would likely gain full marks because it meets all the marking criteria fully (even though it is not a perfect answer).

Now test yourself

TESTED ☐

1 Give one example of a mass audience radio station.
2 Give one example of a niche (or specialist) audience radio station.
3 Explain one way the Radio 1 *Live Lounge* fits the BBC's PSB requirements.
4 Name the media industries term for bringing together different platforms.
5 Name two different platforms that deliver the Radio 1 *Live Lounge.*
6 List four different ways a radio station might offer uses and gratifications.

Answers on p. 133

Music videos

REVISED ☐

Media language

Music video producers use media language to:

- convey the meaning of the song
- promote the artist online and on music television by encouraging replays through visual interest and/or high production values
- promote the producer (e.g. as a means of launching a career as a film director).

The media language can convey the meaning of the song through the tone of the video (e.g. upbeat or dark and sinister, polished and glamorous or street-wise and authentic), which will be determined primarily by the use of mise-en-scène – settings, costume, lighting and colour – performance and narrative, supported by the camerawork and editing.

Music videos as a media form have developed some **generic conventions**. These include such elements as:

- performance to camera
- fast-paced editing
- use of setting or location to express meaning.

> **Generic conventions**: shared elements of a media product, which are repeated so often that they become familiar.

These conventions may be deliberately broken in order to create meaning. For example, some videos have no performance to camera – Fat Boy Slim's 'Ya Mama', for example, does not feature the artist or any performance to camera. This is an example of a *narrative* music video. This might tell the story of the song, or may create a parallel narrative that comments on the meaning of the song, as the Fat Boy Slim video does. Performance videos show the artist singing and/or playing the song, often with dancing, usually with direct address to camera so that the artist appears to be performing for the viewer. Performance videos will sometimes include sections of narrative, performed either by the artist or by actors. Meanwhile, some narrative videos include sections of artists performing, especially towards the end of the video. The set music videos are a mixture of styles, as shown in the table.

Artist	Video style	Artist	Video style
Wheatus	Narrative and performance	Avril Lavigne	Performance plus some narrative
Mark Ronson	Performance	Beyoncé	Narrative plus some performance
The Vamps	Performance	Little Mix	Narrative plus some performance (some to camera)
Tinie Tempah	Performance	Paloma Faith	Narrative plus performance (mostly not to camera)

You should have studied two music videos in detail and should be able to analyse, compare and contrast the media language used in those two set videos, as shown in the table that follows.

Music videos	Media language comparison	Media language contrast
Little Mix – *Black Magic* (*BM*) The Vamps – *Somebody to You* (*STY*)	Both use real locations to connote a sense of naturalism (a sense that we are in real places rather than an artificial environment like a studio). Both bands wear costumes that could be worn every day by teenagers; even when Little Mix become glamorous, the costumes suggest 'ordinary' teenagers dressed up. Both videos include performance to camera. In both videos, the soundtrack is dominated by the music after some diegetic sound at the start. Both videos use a fairly fast editing pace that matches the pace of the song. Both videos are intertextual (they refer to other media products) in that they use locations – the beach party, the high school – established in films, TV and other music videos.	*STY*'s more exotic location (beach/pool) connoting luxury contrasts with *BM*'s 'everyday' school setting, which connotes 'real life'. *STY* is naturalistic throughout; *BM* uses magical elements created partly through special effects to establish a sense of magical transformation (a fantasy element that breaks the sense of 'real life'). *STY*'s hand-held camerawork contrasts with the more controlled camerawork of *BM*. This plus *STY*'s faster editing pace connotes a more 'edgy' feel. *STY*'s narrative based on a performance montage (editing together disparate clips of song and/or dance performance) contrasts with *BM*'s linear narrative (a story with cause and effect) about achieving power in school

Music videos	Media language comparison	Media language contrast
Mark Ronson, Bruno Mars – *Uptown Funk* (*UF*) Beyoncé – *If I Were a Boy* (*IIWAB*)	Both videos have soundtracks dominated by music. Both videos include performance to camera. Both use real American urban locations to connote a sense of naturalism. Both videos use expressive editing transitions, e.g. whip pan edits (cuts as the camera whips rapidly, e.g. at 1'40"), in *UF*, fade to black (e.g. at 3'31") in *IIWAB*. Both videos are intertextual in using 'the street' in ways established by films, TV and other music videos.	In *UF*, the soundtrack consists solely of the song; in *IIWAB* there is diegetic sound interspersed through the song. *UF*'s saturated colour (intense colours) contrasts with the low-contrast monochrome (black and white) for *IIWAB*. *UF*'s use of performance, costume and props (e.g. hair curlers) connotes humour; *IIWAB*'s media language connotes seriousness. *UF*'s use of camerawork connotes performance (e.g. low-angle, wide-angle shots that emphasise movement towards camera); *IIWAB*'s use of camerawork connotes 'realism' by using handheld camera that moves as if held in the hands of a documentary film-maker, and long lens shots with shallow depth of focus (i.e. people and objects other than Beyoncé are out of focus) that look as if they have been captured in the street (e.g. at 1'19"). *UF*'s use of editing emphasises moments in the music, including use of rapid editing, slow motion, 'jump cut dancing' (e.g. at 1'23"), and digital rotation (e.g. at 1'27"), drawing attention to its artificiality; *IIWAB*'s editing is more unobtrusive. *IIWAB*'s linear narrative contrasts with *UF*'s performance montage (editing together disparate clips of song and/or dance performance).

Music videos	Media language comparison	Media language contrast
Tinie Tempah, Jess Glynne – *Not Letting Go* (*NLG*) Paloma Faith – *Picking Up the Pieces* (*PUTP*)	Both use real locations and natural light to connote a sense of naturalism. Both videos include performance to camera. In both videos, the soundtrack is dominated by the music. Both videos use a fairly fast editing pace that matches the pace of the song. Both videos have extensive use of camera movement.	*PUTP*'s linear narrative contrasts with *NLG*'s performance montage. The naturalistic mise-en-scène and social-realist tone for *NLG* contrasts with the more stylised and cinematic mise-en-scène for *PUTP*, e.g. contrasting use of costume and setting (*PUTP*'s rural upmarket setting contrasts with *NLG*'s urban social housing setting). *NLG* uses more exuberant camerawork, e.g. the use of handheld camera and tilts, whereas *PUTP* uses a more formal, cinematic style, with extensive use of framing (e.g. the subject of the shot is placed in a frame created by windows or by columns). *PUTP* is more intertextual in its use of establishing shots of the drive to the country house like a period drama (long distance shots establishing the location, e.g. the drive to the country house).
Music videos	**Media language comparison**	**Media language contrast**
Wheatus – *Teenage Dirtbag* (*TD*) Avril Lavigne – *Sk8er Boi* (*SB*)	Both use real locations to connote a sense of naturalism, added to by the choice of 'everyday' costume for the performers. Both videos include performance to camera. In both videos, the soundtrack is dominated by the music. Both videos make extensive use of camera movement. Both videos use a fairly fast editing pace that matches the pace of the song. Both videos include some linear narrative – that of setting up the concert in *SB* and a fantasy of success with a love interest in *TD*.	The documentary-style mostly hand-held camerawork, desaturated (washed-out) colour and fast-paced editing in *SB* contrasts with the saturated colour, more controlled camerawork and slower-paced editing in *TD* (especially in the narrative sections). The narrative is more clearly developed in *TD*, whereas that in *SB* consists mostly of montage rather than cause and effect. The narrative in *SB* values rebellion, while that in *TD* values 'fitting in' (albeit to an oppressive system). *TD* appears to be set in American suburbia, with its connotations of conformity, whereas *SB* is set in the big city, with its connotations of street credibility. *TD* is more intertextual in its use of a narrative that is familiar from high-school drama.

Revision activity

Watch your two chosen music videos again. Then summarise the two most important points of comparison and contrast in the media language used by the two videos. Note any media language elements you notice that you can add to the table.

Representation

Music video producers use representations to:

- convey the meaning of the song
- promote the artist online and on music television by representing the artist in a way that matches or changes their public image
- promote social messages that reflect well on the artist.

As with media language, you should be able to analyse, compare and contrast the representations in the two set videos you have studied, as shown in the table.

Music videos	Representation comparison	Representation contrast
Little Mix – *Black Magic* (*BM*) The Vamps – *Somebody to You* (*STY*)	Both videos assume the primacy of (heterosexual) love and attraction. Both videos represent the teenage peer group positively, as a source of support and fun. Both videos celebrate youthful 'leisure' values: exuberance, freedom and spontaneity (which *BM* explicitly contrasts to the dullness of maths). Both videos stereotypically represent attractive people as young, thin, white and able-bodied (e.g. the girls on the beach in *STY*, the girl the band compete with in *BM*) Both celebrate a perfect world – a utopia – of exotic beach fun or of teenage takeover in school. Both videos represent the artists as youthful, fun-loving and approachable. Both videos represent stereotypical situations – the beach party, the high school – that are easily recognisable.	*STY* emphasises the male gaze – some women are in the video simply as passive objects of attraction; *BM* has female protagonists and at times represents the female gaze at male objects of attraction or pity. *STY* represents community cohesion, whereas *BM* represents competition between women for male attention (thus re-establishing the importance of the male gaze?). *STY* casts slim, young, white, conventionally attractive actors; *BM* has a wider range of race and ethnicities, body types and ages to suggest a more inclusive message.
Music videos	Representation comparison	Representation contrast
Mark Ronson, Bruno Mars – *Uptown Funk* (*UF*) Beyoncé – *If I Were a Boy* (*IIWAB*)	Both videos assume the primacy of (heterosexual) love and attraction. Both represent masculinity as sexually predatory (though *UF* does this in an ironic way). Both videos represent the US city as an ethnically mixed place of energy, opportunity and drama. Both stereotypically represent attractive people as young, thin and able-bodied. Both *UF* and *IIWAB* deliberately use stereotypes *and* undercut them: *UF* presents stereotypical images of masculine bravado undercut by less stereotypical images of men in curlers; *IIWAB* uses stereotypes of masculine power and feminine victimhood, but undercuts these by inverting them in the first part of the narrative.	*IIWAB*'s representation of a powerful woman with agency (in the first half) contrasts with the explicit sexual objectification of women in *UF*. The *UF* video portrays a self-parody of masculine bragging by deliberate exaggeration and undercutting of the machismo (e.g. by drying hair in curlers alongside a middle-aged woman); the *IIWAB* video is trying to represent a serious message about gender relations. *IIWAB*'s cast of conventionally attractive actors in their adult prime (putting a glamorous gloss on a serious message) contrasts with the cornucopia of different types of actors of all ages in *UF* (creating an insincere but inclusive message).

Music videos	Representation comparison	Representation contrast
Tinie Tempah, Jess Glynne – *Not Letting Go* (*NLG*) Paloma Faith – *Picking Up the Pieces* (*PUTP*)	Both videos assume the primacy of (heterosexual) love, romance and attraction. In both videos, feelings about a personal relationship are externalised in the form of a social setting. Both videos stereotypically represent attractive people as young, thin and able-bodied. Both videos represent Britain as a multicultural society. Both videos represent stereotypical settings – the council estate, the country house hotel – that are easily recognisable.	*NLG* represents street life as an example of community cohesion (a cohesion that reflects a successful personal relationship) whereas *PUTP* represents the difficulties of personal relationships in a social setting concerned with status and impression management. *NLG*'s celebration of youthful exuberance, energy and community contrasts with *PUTP*'s representation of young love as conflict and pain.
Music videos	**Representation comparison**	**Representation contrast**
Wheatus – *Teenage Dirtbag* (*TD*) Avril Lavigne – *Sk8er Boi* (*SB*)	Both videos assume the primacy of (heterosexual) love, romance and attraction – both represent failed love. Both videos celebrate youthful 'leisure' values – exuberance and freedom – at the same time as representing teenage alienation. Both represent the US as a mostly white society. Both represent stereotypical settings – the high school, the big city – that are easily recognisable. Both videos represent the artists as being on the side of the underdog.	*SB*'s representation of a powerful woman with agency (she makes things happen) contrasts with the stereotypical representation of women solely as love objects in *TD*. *SB* celebrates teenage rebellion and rule-breaking, whereas *TD* represents a character trying to conform and succeed. The highly individualistic, status-ridden and competitive world represented in *TD* contrasts with the representation of the solidarity of an outsider community in *SB*.

Revision activity

Watch your two chosen music videos again. Then summarise the two most important points of comparison and contrast in the representations used by the two videos. Note any media language elements you notice that you can add to the table.

Audience identity and interpretation

You should be prepared to discuss:

- the ways in which audiences may interpret the same media products very differently and how those differences may reflect both social and individual differences
- the ways in which people's media practices (uses of the media) are connected to their identity, including their sense of actual and desired self.

Revision activity

Investigate such differences in your class and among people you know. View the comments on your set videos on YouTube and note differences in responses.

Audience interpretation of music videos might depend on a number of differences:

- gender
- sexuality
- race/ethnicity and nationality
- age
- musical taste and fandom
- a wide range of other individual factors and social/cultural contexts.

One reason people have strong reactions to music videos and the artists they represent is the role of popular music in adding to a person's sense of identity. This happens due to a number of factors, such as:

- many audience members become fans of particular artists and this sense of belonging to a group becomes part of their identity
- many audience members can develop a sense of a desired 'outsider' identity by rejecting mainstream pop music and cultivating a taste for less conventional and less popular music
- particular pop songs may 'speak' to audience members at times of heightened emotion (e.g. falling in love, breaking up, having an affair, parenting a child, bereavement) and they may gain a sense of 'owning' that song.

Videos	Identities offered
Little Mix, The Vamps	Young, mid-Atlantic teenage identity
Mark Ronson/Bruno Mars, Beyoncé	Adult, urban, American identity
Tinie Tempah/Jess Glynne, Paloma Faith	Young adult, British identity
Wheatus, Avril Lavigne	American, post-teenage identity

These identities are likely to prompt different responses in different audience members. For example, an American representation might be rejected or used as a means of escape by a British audience.

Revision activity

Investigate the personal identities offered by the two music videos you have studied, using the information in this table as a starting point. Make notes on how the music videos might:

- reinforce a sense of belonging in the world
- reinforce a sense of being a rebel, an outsider, or a member of a special group
- refer to the audience's own powerful personal experiences.

Now test yourself

TESTED

7 State two generic conventions of the music video.
8 State the two forms a music video might take.
9 What term describes a mixing of styles and genres?
10 Why are music videos made?
11 How can audiences use music videos to reinforce their sense of identity?

Answers on p. 133

Magazine audience and industries

REVISED

Ownership

The magazine industry is mostly dominated by publishing companies rather than the very large media conglomerates that own film and television media worldwide. This may be because magazines are struggling in a competitive market and may be best managed by owners who specialise in the print medium. For example, businesses like Bauer and Hearst Communications are still primarily print publishers with some associated television and radio.

As useful background to the industry, the following table is intended to illustrate that magazine publishing is in the hands of a few international companies, an example of **globalisation**. The table includes the paid-for magazines with the highest circulations. Note: you do not need to learn the contents of this table.

> **Globalisation**: the process by which institutions increasingly operate on a worldwide scale.

Magazine	Owner	Business
What's on TV	Time, Inc.	US magazine publisher
Radio Times	Hubert Burda Media	German magazine publisher
TV Choice	Bauer Media	German media conglomerate: magazines, radio and music television
Take a Break	Bauer Media	
Good Housekeeping	Hearst Communications	US media conglomerate: newspapers, magazines, local radio and cable television
Cosmopolitan	Hearst Communications	
BBC Gardeners' World	Hubert Burda Media	German magazine publisher
Vogue	Advance Publications	US newspaper and magazine group

The globalised nature of the magazine industry can be seen in the fact that none of the owners of these 'British' magazines is British.

Mojo is published by Bauer Media. This company owns more than 600 magazines, including two other UK music magazines – *Q* and *Kerrang!*. The company has diversified the *Mojo* brand, offering mojo4music.com online in order to reduce the risk of operating in only one media form. The company is itself diversified, with ownership of magazines, websites, radio stations and music television channels, which may help protect it from declining audiences for magazines.

Revenue

Magazines receive revenue from:
- circulation (cover price £5.25 for *Mojo* in 2017)
- advertising (in *Mojo*, this is mostly for live or recorded music, with some fashion advertising, some mass advertising – e.g. Specsavers – and cross-promotion for other Bauer brands, such as *Empire*)
- sponsored content and **product placement** (payment for showing brands in the editorial content, for example, '*Mojo* listens to all its music on Roksan equipment')
- events, e.g. *Vogue* runs fashion events, *GQ* runs comedy events.

> **Product placement**: when a product is advertised to the audience by being placed in a media product in exchange for payment.

The print magazine industry is suffering from falling advertising revenues and falling circulations as many magazine audiences go online. The response has been to diversify as much as possible – events are a good example of this – and to move magazines online.

Quality monthly magazines

The most successful magazines have been in the quality end of the market – the biggest brands – which offer their audiences what is known as a 'lean back moment': a sense of relaxation as they sink into the glamorous world of their favourite glossy magazines. These magazines use the advantages of the print media – high-quality photography, the ritual consumption of the familiar, and the luxury of sophisticated media language using high-quality printing on glossy paper. They link these to the authoritative brand image of an established magazine. The whole package will attract advertising from high-status brands, which will add to the aspirational, high-quality tone.

Mojo magazine has some aspects of the quality monthly, but it is only semi-glossy and uses lighter-weight paper. However, it retains enough quality to enable it to survive as a paid-for print product while the cheaper weekly music magazines have either closed or, like *NME*, switched to online versions.

Targeting audiences

Weekly magazines tend to have an audience that is more working class than middle class: the paid-for magazines with the highest working-class (C2DE) readership are *Take a Break*, *What's on TV*, *OK!* and *TV Choice* – all weekly magazines.

The quality monthly magazines tend to target a more middle-class audience. The paid-for magazines with the highest middle-class (ABC1) readership are the monthlies *Good Housekeeping*, *Cosmopolitan*, *Vogue* and *BBC Good Food*, followed by the weekly *Radio Times*.

All these most popular weekly and monthly magazines have mostly female readerships. Magazines aimed at men are less successful. The most popular are *Men's Health* and *BBC Top Gear*.

Mojo readers

Mojo had a fairly small circulation of about 68,000 in 2016–2017 and a readership of about 138,000. (For comparison, *Take a Break* and *Cosmopolitan* have readerships of well over 1 million.)

Class:
- *Mojo* gains a similar share of middle-class and working-class readers.

Gender:
- *Mojo* is four times more likely to be read by men than by women.

Age:
- The readership is adult.
- There is a greater number of older readers (over 35) than younger readers: nearly two-thirds of the readers are over 35.
- However, a higher proportion of 15–34 year olds (a much smaller group) read the magazine compared with over 35 year olds (a much bigger group).

Revision activity

Prepare a fact file on *Mojo* magazine's ownership by summarising this material. Visit the Bauer Media website at www.bauermedia.co.uk/ to investigate the other brands owned by this conglomerate.

How to use theory

Uses and Gratifications

The audience may use music magazines for a range of uses and gratifications (see the theory of Blumler and Katz).

Personal identity

- Music magazines often address the fandom of a specialised audience and may reinforce the readers' sense of being a fan of a particular genre of music. For example, *Mojo* magazine addresses educated lovers of 'authentic' music and so might serve to reinforce that identity.
- Music magazines offer aspirational role models – musical stars – with whom their readers may identify. For example, *Mojo* magazine features a 'legendary' musician on the cover every month.

- Music magazines may reinforce a reader's values – either those of the musical genre(s) being celebrated or the valuing of popular culture as a whole. For example, *Mojo* magazine celebrates the values of authenticity and passion associated with 'classic rock' but also celebrates the value of popular music in the seriousness with which it is discussed.

Social interaction and integration

- Music magazines offer news and gossip that might form the basis of real-life conversations. For example, *Mojo* magazine has a regular 'Mind Blowers' section that offers sometimes obscure and edgy recommendations, plus lengthy feature articles that aim to offer original content – both might spark debate.

- Music magazines usually follow a familiar format and offer regular consumption as a form of ritual. For example, *Mojo* magazine has a regular division into 'What goes on', 'Features', 'Filter' and items such as 'All back to my place', 'Theories, rants, etc.', 'Real gone' and 'Hello goodbye'. All these might provide a substitute for real-life interaction in which the magazine is seen by its readers as a good friend.

Entertainment

- Music magazines offer a range of entertainment pleasures, such as comedy, gossip, CDs and other free gifts, striking visuals and attractive stars.
- Music magazines can offer escape into a utopian world of stars, celebrity and pleasure. For example, *Mojo* magazine offers detailed insight into the affairs of bands and artists that may serve as a means of escape from everyday life for its readers.

Surveillance

Music magazines offer a sense of being in contact with the world, giving information about the world of popular music. This is a main function of music magazines. For example, *Mojo* magazine offers:

- 'What goes on' – short articles about music news and current affairs, including possibly unfamiliar material such as 'rising artists' and 'Mind Blowers'
- 'Regulars' include 'Real gone' – obituaries – and 'Ask Fred' – answers to readers' questions
- 'Filter' includes reviews of recorded music, books, TV and film, and live events, plus 'how to buy' – recommendations of the key works by a classic artist.

Audience activity and passivity

Magazines, like all print media, offer a more active audience experience than the audio-visual media forms (TV, film, radio), but a less active experience than the online media. The wide range of choice of publications makes selection a more active process for magazines – audiences can skip through the edition however they like, and most offer readers' letters as a form of feedback.

Audience interpretation

Music magazines are usually niche products, so they aim to address only their specialist audience. The teenage mainstream pop music-loving audience for *We Love Pop* might interpret *Mojo* magazine as hopelessly dull, long-winded and full of old men. The older, classic rock-loving audience for *Mojo* magazine might interpret *We Love Pop* as irrelevant teenage fluff.

Now test yourself

TESTED ☐

12 State how British magazines are globalised.
13 Explain how Bauer Media is diversified.
14 State two ways that a print magazine can gain revenue.
15 Explain how the quality monthly magazines offer an extra audience experience.
16 State one audience category that is more likely to read *Mojo*.
17 List four different ways a music magazine might offer uses and gratifications.

Answers on p. 133

How to prepare for the exam

- Revise what you have learned about music radio, music magazines and music videos as media forms. Explore other music radio stations, music magazines and music videos and note how they are similar to or different from your set products.
- Revise what you have learned about the set products in order to give examples in the exam.

Questions 4 and 5

What these questions involve

REVISED

Question 4 is a 5-mark question requiring analysis of:
- either: an extract from *Mojo* magazine printed in the exam paper
- or: one or both of your set music videos (no extract in the exam paper).

This is an analysis question so can ask about media language and representation only.

Question 5 is a 15-mark question requiring analysis that compares the media language in extracts from two magazines, one of which will be *Mojo* magazine.

Timing

REVISED

Question 4 is a short essay question that should take about five minutes.

Question 5 is an extended essay question that should take about 15 minutes.

What the examiner is looking for

REVISED

The examiner is looking for answers to both questions that show sophisticated, perceptive and accurate analysis that focuses on the area – media language or representation – used in the extract (or the set product if asking about a music video).

In Question 5, the examiner is further looking for the student to make judgements and reach conclusions.

Exam tip

Making judgements and reaching conclusions may be best done by ending with a paragraph that comes to a conclusion, even though you may have made judgements throughout the answer. You might signal this by starting the paragraph with 'In conclusion…'. The words 'How far' at the beginning of the question are a further pointer to your need to make judgements.

Exam practice

Question 4

Analyse the representations of musicians in the extract from *Mojo* magazine. [5]

Question 5*

How far is media language used differently in the extracts from *Mojo* and *We Love Pop* magazines to reflect genre conventions? In your answer you must:
- analyse examples of how media language is used differently in the extracts from *Mojo* and *We Love Pop* magazines
- make judgements and reach conclusions about whether there are more similarities due to genre conventions than differences in the extracts.

The magazine extracts may be found at www.ocr.org.uk/Images/316661-unit-j200-02-music-and-news-sample-assessment-material.pdf [15]

* See p. 86.

Extended response questions

The asterisk (★) next to Question 5 is to signpost that this is an extended response answer, meaning that you will be marked on the quality of your essay:

● how well you develop a line of reasoning
● how relevant your answer is throughout
● how well you provide evidence for the points you make.

Bullet-pointed questions

The bullet points in Question 5 tell you exactly what the examiners are looking for in your answer – they state everything you have to do to meet the demands of the mark scheme.

'Full course of study' questions

Sometimes – though not in this case – Question 5 may start with this phrase:

● 'In this question you will be rewarded for drawing together elements from your full course of study, including different areas of the theoretical frameworks and media contexts.'

This statement will occur once in each exam paper at the beginning of a 15-mark question (so in this paper it could come before Question 5 or Question 9). The statement means you must cover more than one of the four areas of the theoretical framework – media language, representations, industries and audiences – to achieve the top of the highest mark band.

In Question 5 it would mean that you should cover one other area as well as media language. For example, you could discuss how the differences in media language in the two extracts fit the different target audiences of the two products. The two areas do not have to be covered at equal length; just one point from a second area is enough.

> *Mojo* is aimed at a grown-up audience while *We Love Pop* is aimed at a teenage audience, so they make their front covers appeal to those audiences by using different media language. *Mojo* has more sophisticated media language that connotes quality; *We Love Pop* has media language that connotes fun.

> If this question did ask for coverage of more than one area of the theoretical framework then this audience point would count as a second area in addition to media language. This means that the answer could access the full range of marks available.

Making judgements and reaching conclusions

If a question asks 'how far' something is true or you agree with a statement, this should be the focus of your conclusion. In Question 5 you might argue one of the following:

● There are more similarities than differences and these are due to genre conventions.
● There are more similarities than differences but these are not due to genre conventions.
● There are more differences than similarities.
● There are an equal number of similarities and differences.

Revision activity

Can you think of any other points about media audiences, representations or industries that you could use to explain the differences in media language between the two extracts?

Examiners will be told to credit any argument that is backed up by analysis of the extract, so there is no 'right answer' to these questions with which you have to agree. You should carry out your analysis first and then make your decision later, basing this on the evidence. Analyse the sample answer below.

> There are more differences than similarities between the two front covers. Both have mastheads at the top of the page but so do all other magazines. They both have cover lines but so do all other magazines. These similarities are not due to them being music magazines. They are very different because they are about different kinds of music that appeal to different audiences.

> It is difficult to judge this conclusion on its own as markers are looking to see how well it is supported by the previous analysis. However, it is likely that this would be at the top of Level 2 – as a 'partially clear judgement and conclusion'.

Exam tip

You do not always have to come down on one side or the other in a debate – you can argue that both sides are partially correct or that the situation is more nuanced than the question suggests.

Contexts

One analysis question across Papers 1 and 2 will ask you to refer to media contexts in your answer. This might be Question 4 or Question 5 in this section. You may be able to apply one of the following social/cultural contexts:

- **changes in gender roles**
- **changing attitudes to sexualities**
- **multiculturalism**
- **celebrity culture**
- **consumerism**.

Question 4 could ask you to analyse the media language and/or representations in a magazine extract or the two set music videos you have studied. The extract from a magazine is likely to be from *Mojo* but could be the second magazine extract for Question 5 that is not *Mojo* magazine. For this question you need to revise the media language and representations in the two music videos you have studied and practise analysing the media language and representations in magazines, especially *Mojo*.

Question 5 will ask you to compare media language in two extracts, so you need to practise analysing the media language in magazines, especially *Mojo*.

Media language and representations in music videos

REVISED

You will need to be completely familiar with your chosen two music videos so that you can answer an analysis question in the exam.

An analysis question like Question 4 will just ask you to analyse only your set music videos. Questions 2 or 3 are knowledge and understanding questions, so they could ask about music videos as a media form, but you

Revision activity

- Can you think of any ways to improve this conclusion?
- Can you think of any opposing arguments, i.e. that there are similarities due to genre?

Changes in gender roles/ changing attitudes to gender: the increasing role of women in public life (e.g. politics) following the impact of 1970s feminism.

Changing attitudes to sexualities: the increasingly visible role of LGBT people in public life and acceptance of different sexualities.

Multiculturalism: the change from a white society in which racism is 'normal' to one characterised by many different racial and ethnic groups.

Celebrity culture: the organisation of popular culture around celebrities – people who are famous for being famous.

Consumerism: the expectation that people will aspire to 'better themselves' by buying goods and services (e.g. clothes, cars, houses) that mark out their individual identity. (Opposing ideas to consumerism may include: to reject material goods or to follow one's duty to a group or society.)

might need your music video analysis for these questions as well to use as examples. This is why media language and representations have been covered under Questions 2 and 3.

For media language, you should analyse the connotations of:
- camerawork – e.g. distinctive shots or camera movement, handheld versus controlled, **monochrome** versus colour
- editing – e.g. pace, effects, distinctive juxtapositions
- mise-en-scène – e.g. use of setting/location, lighting, costume, performance
- soundtrack (if there is any **diegetic sound** alongside the song, or use of silence)
- how the media language creates a narrative – e.g. **montage or linear narrative**, **Proppian heroes and villains**
- how the media language portrays aspects of reality, presents a point of view and represents the world to create messages and values – e.g. what is celebrated or criticised by the media language
- the generic conventions of music videos (including hybridity between performance and narrative videos)
- uses of **intertextuality** in music videos.

You can use the content of the tables on music videos and media language under Questions 2 and 3 in any analysis question, together with your own insights.

For representations, you should analyse:
- how the producers have chosen to construct a version of reality that represents events, social groups and ideas to fit their purposes
- how and why stereotypes have been used (e.g. to enable quick interpretation by audiences)
- which social groups are under-represented or misrepresented
- the messages and values conveyed and issues addressed.

You can use the content of the tables on music videos and representations under Questions 2 and 3 in any analysis question, together with your own insights.

Analysis questions can also ask about contexts:
- how these representations reflect their social/cultural contexts.

Media contexts and representations

In your analysis you may need to discuss how the music videos reflect their social/cultural contexts. Some contexts apply across all music videos. For example:
- the centrality of a key performer or performers in each video reflects contemporary celebrity culture – the celebrity performer promotes their song and the song promotes their celebrity
- each music video reflects consumerism – the idea that we express ourselves in our consumer choices, including clothing and lifestyle.

Some contexts apply particularly to certain videos:
- The Little Mix *Black Magic* video reflects multiculturalism (in its racial and ethnic mix) and the influence of feminism (in its celebration of 'girl power') in modern Britain, whereas The Vamps *Somebody to You* video does not appear to reflect either.
- Both the Mark Ronson, Bruno Mars *Uptown Funk* and Beyoncé *If I Were a Boy* videos reflect multiculturalism in their racial and ethnic mix, but *IIWAB* reflects changing attitudes to gender with an

---

Monochrome: one colour; usually means black and white.

Diegetic sound: sound from within the fictional world – it would be heard by the characters if they were real.

Montage narrative: a number of shots put together where the earlier shots do not cause the later ones but are more like a list.

Linear narrative: a narrative where earlier events cause later events; A leads to B, which leads to C, and so on. Usually has a beginning, middle and end.

Proppian heroes and villains: Propp's theory was that narratives share similar characters, such as heroes, villains, princesses, dispatcher, and so on. This was based on studying folk tales but applies to many media products.

Intertextuality: references to other media products that are expected to be recognised by the audience.

explicitly feminist message about mistreatment of women, whereas *UF* is not feminist in its depiction of female sex objects but does suggest some changing attitudes to sexualities alongside the male bragging.

- Both the Tinie Tempah, Jess Glynne *Not Letting Go* and Paloma Faith *Picking Up the Pieces* videos reflect multiculturalism in their racial and ethnic mix, but *PUTP* reflects changing attitudes to gender with an explicitly feminist message about female attractiveness and objectification whereas *NLG* does not.
- The Avril Lavigne *Sk8er Boi* video reflects changing attitudes to gender with its powerful female lead character, whereas the Wheatus *Teenage Dirtbag* video does not, with its objectification of women.

Media language analysis of magazines

REVISED

You should have practised analysing music magazines and comparing the media language in *Mojo* and one other magazine in preparation for Question 5.

For media language, you should analyse:

- layout – e.g. any distinctive use of layout, the proportion of space, image and copy, the use of cluttered or ordered layout, the use of symmetrical and asymmetrical layout, house style
- typography – e.g. **serif and sans serif typefaces**, specialist typefaces, bold, italics
- colour – e.g. tones, saturation, house style
- images – e.g. graphics, camerawork and mise-en-scène in photography, digital manipulation
- use of language – e.g. **formal and informal registers, direct mode of address**, puns, colloquialisms, slang
- how the media language portrays aspects of reality, presents a point of view and represents the world to create messages and values – e.g. what is celebrated or criticised by the media language
- how the magazine uses the advantages of print technology – e.g. **colour saturation,** glossy presentation, detailed copy (writing)
- the **generic conventions** of music magazines – e.g. front cover dominated by images of musicians, style of the magazine reflects the genre of music, magazine assumes and addresses the audience's fandom
- use of intertextuality in music magazines – e.g. references to other media products.

Connotations

For each element of media language you analyse, you should discuss its connotations. Here are some typical examples:

> **Serif and sans serif typefaces**: a typeface is a family of fonts. Serif typefaces have small ornaments called serifs. Sans serif typefaces don't, so they look cleaner and more modern, whereas serif typefaces look more traditional.

> **Formal and informal registers**: a formal language register is used in formal situations, conveys information, uses more complex language and is impersonal. An informal register is used in social situations, establishes a relationship, uses slang and simpler language, and is personal.

> **Direct mode of address**: for example, where a sentence uses the word 'you' or a person looks into the camera.

> **Colour saturation**: the richness of the colour. A saturated colour is the opposite of a pastel colour.

> **Generic conventions**: shared elements of a media product, which are repeated so often that they become familiar.

Element	Examples	Typical connotations
Layout	Cluttered layout	Informality, plenty, energy
	Ordered layout	Formality, authority, organisation
Typography	Serif fonts	Tradition, formality, sophistication
	Sans serif fonts	Modernity, informality, no-nonsense
Colour	Saturated primary colours	Energy, youthfulness, brightness
	Muted colour mixes	Sophistication, elegance
Use of language	Formal register	Formality, objectivity, authority
	Informal register, with direct address and colloquialisms	Personal connection, sharing, brashness

You should always remember that the connotations of use of media language depend on the combination of elements in any product, so the connotations may vary from one product to another even if aspects of the media language remain the same.

If we take the *Mojo* and *We Love Pop* extracts as an example:

Media language element	Mojo	Connotation	We Love Pop	Connotation
Layout	Ordered content with the cover lines mostly aligned and one central image	Seriousness, authenticity	Cluttered layout with use of diagonals and irregular boxes	Plenty, excitement
Typography	Exclusively sans serif typefaces and capitalisation used	Modernity	Sans serif typefaces used with capitalisation, shadowing and specialist fonts such as the 'drip' effect	Youth, vitality and fun
Colour	Palette is mostly limited to black and white plus touches of muted red and yellow	Black background for sophistication and elegance	Palette includes neon pink and saturated blue	Youthful femininity
Image	Main image uses monochrome photography – a three-quarters close-up with low-key side lighting; subject does not address the camera	Documentary realism	Multitude of images mostly with artificial floodlighting, variety of angles from close-up to medium long shot, all with direct address	Plenty and engagement in the manner of social media
Language	Language emphasises difficulty and danger: 'torment', 'society tried to extinguish me', 'surviving the Kinks', 'living dangerously'	Serious lives looked at in a wry manner	Language emphasises revelations: 'crush cringes and dating disasters!', 'my crazy world', 'our Instagram secrets revealed'	Connection with the teenage world of the target audience
Portraying reality	The media language presents a world that celebrates serious artistic endeavour		The media language presents a world that celebrates fun, romance and celebrity	
Technology	The page uses print to produce a rich black		The page uses print to produce saturated colour	
Generic conventions	The front cover is dominated by an image of a musician; the serious style of the magazine reflects the values of fans of 'classic rock'; the magazine assumes and addresses the audience's fandom for the artists on the cover		The front cover is dominated by images of musicians; the excited style of the magazine reflects the values of fans of young teenage pop; the magazine assumes and addresses the audience's fandom for the artists on the cover. The cover suggests that the magazine is a hybrid between a music magazine and a lifestyle magazine, with content about dates and fashion	
Intertextuality	'Year of living dangerously', 'Dark Knight' and 'Angels and demons' are all references to books and films		References social media platforms and *The Lego Batman Movie*	

Representation analysis of magazines

You may be asked to perform a representation analysis in Question 4. You could be asked to analyse representations generally or in relation to specific groups such as musicians, gender, race and ethnicity, age and so on, or even to events and ideas. The group would need to be present clearly on the front cover for you to be asked to analyse it.

Representation analysis includes:

● how the producers have chosen to construct a version of reality that represents events, social groups and ideas to fit their purposes
● how and why stereotypes have been used (e.g. to enable quick interpretation); this includes anti-stereotyping (also known as counter-stereotyping)
● which social groups are under-represented or misrepresented
● the messages and values conveyed and the issues addressed
● how these representations reflect their social/cultural contexts.

If we take the *Mojo* extract as an example:

How the producers have chosen to construct a version of reality that represents events, social groups and ideas to fit their purposes	*Mojo* wishes to attract a target audience that shares its reverence for 'classic rock' so constructs a version of reality that represents musicians as authentic heroes, striving for excellence, e.g. in the photo of Ray Davies looking towards the heavens framed by a black background
How and why stereotypes have been used	The selection of a cover photograph of a young, white male may be to fit the stereotype of rock musicians. There is an anti-stereotypical positive representation of older people as popular musicians, e.g. the artist from CSNY on the front cover – this may reflect the anti-ageism of an older audience.
Which social groups are under-represented or misrepresented	The front cover represents only white male musicians in photographs under-representing females and musicians of colour.
The messages and values conveyed and the issues addressed	The front cover associates musicians with quest, danger and struggle, celebrating the values associated with rock music of 'living fast and dying young'.
How these representations reflect their social/cultural contexts	The representations reflect the dominance of celebrity culture in society. They reflect the continuing significance of a 1960s generation who developed popular music in a period of social upheaval.

Read the Exam practice Question 4 on page 86 again and answer the question yourself in five minutes. Look at the full sample response below.

This front cover of *Mojo* magazine fits the stereotype of rock musicians as serious artists who grapple with serious themes. Language such as 'Arise! Ray Davies' and use of the term 'legends' suggests a reverence towards the musicians that fits the purpose of the magazine's producers – to sell a celebration of 'classic rock' to fans of the genre.

The way they are represented associates musicians with quest, danger and struggle in a way that fits this stereotype. For example, the 'black and white photograph of a young Ray Davies looking towards the heavens combined with the cover line 'Rock's dark knight on surviving the Kinks and saving his soul' connotes a spiritual quest. Language use such as 'their year of living dangerously', 'KLF burn again', 'the torment of ...' again connotes danger and struggle. This is all done in an ironic way in order to avoid appearing too self-important.

The selection of white male musicians as front cover images fits the mostly white stereotype of rock musicians. However, positive representations of older people as rock musicians may be seen as an anti-stereotype, e.g. the artist from CSNY dominates the frame in a way that suggests he has power and authority. By contrast, the selection of an old photograph of Ray Davies in his youth to may suggest a stereotypical preference for youthful images of rock musicians.

This is a Level 3 answer (4–5 marks) as it is:
- a sophisticated analysis of relevant aspects of the extract
- a highly relevant response to the question, demonstrated by full focus on how media representations are used in the extract.

It would probably gain full marks because it meets all the marking criteria fully (not because it is a perfect answer).

Now read the Exam practice Question 5 on page 86 again and answer the question yourself in 15 minutes. A full sample response is laid out below.

There are a number of differences in the use of media language in the two magazine extracts. Colour is used differently: the use of neon pink in We Love Pop connotes playfulness and femininity, whereas the use of black in Mojo connotes seriousness and authenticity. The cluttered layout of We Love Pop with a range of images and little column alignment contrasts with the more ordered layout in Mojo, dominated by one large central image and aligned columns. The We Love Pop layout connotes fullness and variety, Mojo's layout connotes order and sophistication. The relative demotion of the masthead on We Love Pop contrasts with the banner masthead of Mojo, suggesting that the Mojo brand is to be treated with more respect. The highly stylised typography in We Love Pop (e.g. the dripping 'Love Sucks') connotes a silliness that is the opposite of the more conventional typography in Mojo. The more informal language use suggesting commonality of experience in We Love Pop (e.g. 'decode his Snapchat', 'Crush Cringes & Dating Disasters') links to the hybridity of the magazine – both music and lifestyle – whereas the use of language in Mojo to suggest the speaker's different experience (e.g. 'Society tried to extinguish me') fits the music magazine genre. The photographs are very different: there are many conventionally lit photographs in We Love Pop, making it look like a scrapbook, but one main, chiaroscuro lit, photograph in Mojo, giving it a more artistic feel.

Despite these differences there are a number of similarities in the two extracts, such as: both feature a range of musicians on the front cover, either in cover lines or images; both use language to try to create an inclusive mode of address, addressing an audience of music fans. These are generic conventions of the music magazine. Both use a range of sans serif fonts – this is a style decision rather than a generic convention. Both have mastheads at the top of the page and cover lines – these are common features to all magazines and not due to genre.

In conclusion, there are many differences and some similarities. Some similarities are die to genre conventions, but the differences between the two front covers far outweigh these similarities. However, some of these differences may be due to generic hybridity – the use of lifestyle magazine conventions in We Love Pop. Some of the differences may be due to the difference in the genres of music being covered – We Love Pop can be seen to follow the conventions of the pop music magazine sub-genre, whereas Mojo follows the conventions of the rock music magazine sub-genre. This means that the differences can be due to genre conventions as well as the similarities.

This answer would gain a Level 3 mark (11–15 marks) because:
● it is a sophisticated analysis of relevant examples of media language used in *We Love Pop* and *Mojo* supported by two or more detailed examples
● a clear judgement and conclusion is reached and is fully supported by the analysis.
It would probably gain full marks because it meets all the marking criteria fully (even though it is not a perfect answer).

Now test yourself

TESTED

1 State whether this is an example of a serif or sans serif font: F
2 State one connotation of this kind of font.
3 State whether this is an example of a serif or sans serif font: F
4 State one connotation of this kind of font.
5 Name three social/cultural contexts used in this chapter.
6 Define 'intertextuality'.
7 Define 'generic hybridity'.

Answers on p. 134

How to prepare for the exam

● Practise analysing and comparing music magazine front covers in terms of media language and representations. Analyse one or two inside pages from *Mojo* as well.
● Compare the media language in a wide range of music magazines to that in *Mojo*, e.g. jazz, folk, classical, hip hop and pop music magazines.

What you have to do

This section of the exam asks five questions on your study of news across two media forms:

● an in-depth study of online newspapers, with the *Observer* magazine as the set product
● a study of print newspapers, with the *Observer* as the set product, including both contemporary and historical newspapers from the 1960s.

Which areas of the theoretical framework must I study?	
Online newspapers	The whole theoretical framework: ● media language ● media representations ● industries ● audiences Social/cultural and political contexts
Print newspapers	Media industries Media language Representations Social/cultural, political and historical contexts

The five questions will be as follows:

Q6	1 mark	This question will ask for knowledge and you should write a very short answer.
Q7	4 marks	This question will ask for knowledge and understanding, so your answer should be at least two sentences, taking about four minutes to answer.
Q8	5 marks	This question will ask you to analyse an extract in the exam paper from one of the following: ● the print *Observer* ● the *Observer* website (PC, tablet or mobile versions) ● the *Guardian*'s 'Comment is free' section ● the *Guardian*'s Twitter or Instagram feeds. This question will ask you to analyse the media language or representations in the extract, taking about five minutes to answer. It may ask you to refer to contexts.
Q9	15 marks	This question will ask you to analyse an extract in the exam paper from one of the following: ● the print *Observer* ● the *Observer* website ● the *Guardian*'s 'Comment is free' section ● the *Guardian*'s Twitter or Instagram feeds. This question will ask you to analyse the media language and/or representations in the extract and come to a judgement and conclusion about them. This longer essay should take about 15 minutes to answer. It may ask you to refer to contexts.
Q10	10 marks	This question will ask for knowledge and understanding of how media contexts influence newspapers. It will ask you to give examples from the *Observer* from the 1960s and/or from recent editions.

Question 6

What this question involves

This is a 1-mark knowledge-only question about newspapers, so can cover any area of the theoretical framework, including media industries and audiences.

Timing

This is a short question that should take less than one minute.

What the examiner is looking for

Examiners are looking for correct answers. The answer might be something such as: a definition of a key term, a fact about the media industries, the name of a regulator.

Exam practice

Question 6

Identify one element of press freedom. [1]

For this question you will revise:
- factual questions – these are likely to be about media industries, but any area could come up in this question
- media industries – you should revise facts about regulation and ownership and the meaning of key terms.

Media industries facts for newspapers

Media regulators	
Newspapers	Independent Press Standards Organisation (IPSO) or IMPRESS
	The *Guardian* and the *Observer* have not signed up to either regulator and remain self-regulating (as of November 2017)
	Most other national print newspapers and their websites have signed up to IPSO
Media owners for set products	
Observer	The Guardian Media Group, owned by the Scott Trust

Now test yourself

1 Identify the owner of the *Observer*.
2 Identify one regulator for newspapers.
3 Audiences can read newspapers online using a computer, tablet or mobile phone. What is the term for this use of different platforms for the same content?

Answers on p. 134

How to prepare for the exam

- Create a glossary of all the key terms you use as part of the course, with a definition of each one. Learn any media industries and audiences key terms.
- Create a list of the regulators for each of the media forms you study and memorise the list.
- Learn the name of the owners of the *Guardian* and the *Observer*.

Question 7

What this question involves

Question 7 is a 4-mark knowledge and understanding question about print and/or online news, so can cover any area of the theoretical framework, including media industries and audiences.

Timing

Question 7 is a short question that should take about four minutes.

What the examiner is looking for

Examiners are looking for answers that show knowledge and understanding of specific areas of the theoretical framework – media language, representations, industries or audiences – applied to newspapers. If the question asks you to refer to the set product you have studied, then you must do so, using it as an example to help answer the question.

The question might ask you for two explanations or one explanation and one example for the 4 marks.

If the question asks for two explanations, the examiners would then be looking for two clear explanations (one sentence each) for 4 marks. Very short statements (perhaps only one word) would gain only 1 mark, if they were accurate.

If the question asks for one explanation and one example, the examiner would be looking for a clear explanation (one sentence) for 2 marks and an appropriate example for 2 marks.

Exam practice

Question 7

Explain why a newspaper would shut down its print edition and go online only. Give one example of a newspaper that has done this. [4]

Example 1

A newspaper might shut down its print edition because it costs money to print the newspaper and send it out to newsagents so they can't make a profit if sales are too low. *The Independent* newspaper is one example of a print newspaper that is now online only.

This answer has a clearly explained reason and an accurate example, so earns 4 marks.

Example 2

To save money.

This answer has stated one reason, rather than explaining it, so earns 1 mark. There is no example given.

Exam practice

Question 7

Explain two ways that newspapers are funded. [4]

Example 1

One way newspapers are funded is by selling advertising space, either in the print edition or online – advertisers will pay to display their ads in an authoritative location.

A second way newspapers are funded is by charging readers to view some of a newspaper's content online – a paywall. This works best for newspapers with quality content that readers are happy to pay for, such as the Financial Times.

Two ways of funding newspapers are clearly explained, so 2 marks would be given for each explanation. The question does not ask for examples, so the reference to the *Financial Times* is not really needed; the answer could earn full marks without an example, though it does help establish the explanation.

Example 2

Newspapers sell advertising and cost money to buy.

Two ways are just about stated but not explained, so 1 mark for each would be awarded.

Factual questions are likely to be about media industries, but any area could come up in this question. For media industries, you should revise facts about regulation and ownership and the meaning of key terms.

Broadsheet and tabloid newspapers

REVISED

The terms **broadsheet** and **tabloid** are still in common use to describe the style of a newspaper, although few newspapers are still printed in the broadsheet format (two Sunday newspapers – *The Sunday Times* and *Sunday Telegraph* – are still broadsheets, the *Observer* is now tabloid size). The 'quality' or 'broadsheet' press sometimes refer to their tabloid format as 'compact', as they feel the term 'tabloid' carries negative connotations of sensationalism and gutter journalism.

Broadsheet: literally, a large-sized newspaper (about twice the size of a tabloid), but now used to describe the 'quality press', newspapers that cover mostly 'hard' or serious news stories, such as politics, business, foreign affairs, even though most of these newspapers are now changing to tabloid size, e.g. *The Times*, the *Telegraph*, the *Guardian*, the *Observer*, *Financial Times*.

Tabloid: literally, a small-sized newspaper (about half the size of a broadsheet), but now used to describe newspapers that court popularity by sensationalism, and 'soft' news stories about scandal, celebrities and the entertainment business, e.g. *Daily Mirror* and *Sun*.

The generic conventions of tabloid and broadsheet newspapers are outlined below.

Tabloid	Broadsheet
Softer news agenda, e.g. human interest stories, celebrities	Harder news agenda, e.g. politics, finance, international news
Less formal language register	More formal language register
Pages dominated by headlines and images	Pages dominated by copy
Targets a more downmarket audience	Targets a more upmarket audience
Offers news as entertainment	Offers news as information

This simple division does not always work in practice:
- Newspapers such as the *Daily Mail* position themselves as mid-market, combining conventions of both the tabloid and broadsheets.
- Some traditionally 'tabloid' features, such as extensive use of photography, human interest stories and stories about celebrities, are increasingly common in the broadsheet press, especially in supplements such as the *Guardian*'s *G2*.

The following newspapers are considered the 'quality press' or 'broadsheets':
- *The Times* and *Sunday Times*
- the *Daily Telegraph* and the *Sunday Telegraph*
- the *Guardian* and the *Observer*
- the *i*
- the *Financial Times*.

The following newspapers are considered the 'popular press' or 'red top tabloids':
- the *Sun* and the *Sun on Sunday*
- the *Daily Mirror* and *Sunday Mirror*
- the *Daily Star* and *Daily Star Sunday*.

Two other newspapers titles are considered to be 'middle-market tabloids':
- the *Daily Mail* and *Mail on Sunday*
- the *Daily Express* and *Sunday Express*.

These lie in between the quality press and red-top tabloids in that they deliver more hard news than the other tabloids (though this is less true of the Express newspapers) and their media language is a **hybrid** of tabloid and broadsheet conventions.

Funding

Traditionally, print newspapers depended on circulation and advertising for revenue. Tabloid newspapers like the *Daily Mirror* had larger circulations but working-class audiences that were less attractive to advertisers, so relied more on cover price; broadsheet newspapers had the reverse – smaller circulations but attractive upmarket audiences – and relied more on advertising.

Newspapers now have a wider range of funding sources:
- the cover price of the newspaper
- **paywalls** – paying to access online content, e.g. at the *Times* and *Telegraph* websites; the *Sun* has recently discontinued this option as it reduces online readership

Hybrid: a media product that combines a number of different genres.

Paywall: denies access to a website without a payment.

- contributors: members, subscribers and donators – the *Guardian/Observer* are experimenting with this model for protecting free online content. They announced that they had reached 800,000 paying contributors worldwide in October 2017 and that the income from this now exceeded that from advertising
- print and online advertising – print is traditionally much more lucrative than online advertising but has drastically reduced in recent years, while online newspapers reach a global audience and can sell advertising to different national audiences (the *Guardian* accessed in Greece, for example, carries advertising aimed at Greeks in the Greek language)
- sponsored content – brands supplying content and/or paying to be connected to content, e.g. in the *Guardian*, 'Cricket has no boundaries' paid for and controlled by the bank NatWest, or 'Connecting Britain', editorially independent content 'supported by' Alstom, the train company – in the first example the advertiser has supplied the content, in the second the *Guardian* has supplied the content but the advertiser has agreed to pay to 'support' it
- events – the *Guardian/Observer* frequently run courses (e.g. on journalism or literature), meetings and conferences
- product sales – the *Guardian/Observer* sell holidays and books, for example, linked to their review and travel sections.

Print and online newspapers

REVISED

All print newspapers are facing declining circulations at the same time as much advertising is moving online. Online versions of newspapers attract online advertising, but this is both worth less than print advertising and mostly goes to Facebook and Google. Print newspapers are facing a crisis. Once circulation dips below a certain level – 100,000 copies, for example – it becomes too expensive to physically print newspapers. Hence, one national newspaper, the *Independent*, went online only in 2016.

Newspapers try to avoid going online only as the print version carries the authority of the traditional news source:

- It is feared that a newspaper will lose its influence if it becomes just another website.
- A print version is still seen as an essential promotional tool for online versions of newspapers – it will be seen on television in news round-ups, in shops, in people's hands.

As more readers rely on social media sites such as Facebook and Twitter for their news, these become an important 'shop window' for newspapers – those with readily recognised brands that are trusted may attract readers who are concerned about 'fake news'.

> **Revision activity**
>
> Look at the range of funding sources for newspapers.
> 1 Which of these makes the newspaper more dependent on advertisers?
> 2 Which of these makes the newspaper less dependent on advertising?
> 3 Which of these are made possible or easier by online newspapers?

Newspaper industries – ownership and control

REVISED

Newspapers are not usually profitable but are seen as a means of gaining political and social influence, so are often owned by rich individuals rather than **conglomerates**. Newspaper-owning businesses tend to specialise in newspaper (and sometimes magazine) publishing rather than a range of media.

> **Conglomerate**: a large (often multinational) business organisation that owns a number of different companies.

The *Guardian* and the *Observer*

The *Guardian* and the *Observer* are owned by a trust set up in the 1930s, the Scott Trust. This owns Guardian Media Group, which runs the newspaper. The Scott Trust exists to:

● ensure the editorial independence of the newspapers
● appoint their editors
● ensure the newspapers continue their liberal traditions and do not affiliate to any political party
● promote the cause of **freedom of the press**.

These liberal values mean that the *Guardian* and the *Observer* believe in a tolerant and caring society and tend to support the Labour or Liberal Democratic parties at elections.

History of the *Observer*

The *Observer* was a similarly liberal newspaper before the Guardian Media Group bought it in 1993. It underwent a potentially disastrous ownership in the 1970s when it was used as a weapon in the owner's vendetta against a business rival. The editor from that time now claims that the owner threatened to close down the newspaper unless he pulled an article that might damage the owner's business interests in Zimbabwe. The *Observer* is the world's oldest Sunday newspaper, dating back to 1791, and this was an attack on its journalistic ethics and integrity. This could not happen now as the Scott Trust was set up precisely to avoid that kind of situation.

How much control do owners have?

Owners are not expected to interfere blatantly with the newspaper. Direct interference might destroy the newspaper's credibility, as in the case of the *Observer*, and will be resisted by editors and journalists. Editors who are interviewed in the media routinely deny that their owner interferes with their newspaper's content. However, the owner will appoint the editor, so they can appoint people with similar views to their own.

Political contexts

Owners can enjoy political influence. The Leveson Inquiry into the press found that politicians of all parties had 'developed too close a relationship with the press in a way that has not been in the public interest' and that politicians' relationships with newspaper owners, managers and editors were not clear and open.

Newspapers have influence as one of their roles is to express strong, biased opinion about political policies – unlike, for example, the BBC, which is supposed to be **impartial** and unbiased. One way a policy can be tested is by announcing it to the press and waiting for their reaction. Conservative policy-makers wouldn't want condemnation from **right-wing** papers such as the *Mail* or *Telegraph*; Labour policy-makers wouldn't want condemnation from **left-wing** papers such as the *Observer*, *Guardian* and *Mirror*.

Press freedom and regulation

REVISED

Newspapers were the main form of mass communication at the time when Britain was becoming a full democracy, where all adults had the vote. A free press was seen as crucial to democracy – censorship was

> **Freedom of the press**: anyone must be free to set up a newspaper and newspapers must not be censored or otherwise controlled by the state, in order to provide democratic freedom of expression; state-controlled newspapers are associated with dictatorships.

> **Impartial**: news that tries to present both sides of an issue.
>
> **Right wing**: right wingers in politics (e.g. the Conservatives) believe in a smaller state, lower taxes and more freedom for business.
>
> **Left wing**: left wingers in politics (e.g. the Labour Party) believe in a larger state, more spending to provide welfare, and more state control over the economy.

abolished and press freedom came to be seen as a precious ideal to be defended at all costs. Anyone must be free to set up a newspaper and newspapers must be allowed to publish whatever they want without interference from the government or other authorities.

This ideal of press freedom remains very much alive today and is the reason why newspapers and magazines are not regulated by a body set up by the government (such as Ofcom, which regulates television).

Invasion of privacy

The 'red top' or 'tabloid' press have a brash, no-nonsense style that has led to regular concerns about issues such as invasion of privacy. Matters came to a head when the *Guardian* exposed the Sunday newspaper the *News of the World* as having hacked the voicemails of a young murder victim. This 'hacking scandal' led to the newspaper's closure (it was replaced by the *Sun on Sunday*) and the Leveson Inquiry into the press.

The Leveson Inquiry recommended that the press should regulate itself but that this body would have to be recognised by a panel set up by parliament to make sure it 'had teeth'. In response, most of the press joined a new regulator named IPSO (Independent Press Standards Organisation), which refused to apply to the panel as it saw this as state interference in the free press. A rival regulator, IMPRESS, has been acknowledged by the recognition body but has not recruited any national print newspapers. The *Observer* and the *Guardian* had not joined either body as of November 2017.

Online news is not regulated at all, unless online newspapers choose to sign up to a regulator. The issue of 'fake news' came to prominence particularly during and after the 2016 US presidential election and the British Brexit referendum, especially with regards to Twitter and Facebook. Newspapers such as the *Guardian/Observer* try to offer a trusted brand online by applying the same ethics and journalistic practices as the print newspapers and by actively moderating readers' comments to filter out inappropriate comments.

> **Revision activity**
>
> Look at news reports from the BBC, for example, about 'fake news' and manipulation of public opinion by using Facebook and Twitter. For example,
> - www.theguardian.com/ politics/2017/nov/13/ theresa-may-accuses-russia-of-interfering-in-elections-and-fake-news
> - www.bbc.co.uk/news/ education-41902914
> - www.theguardian.com/ media/2016/dec/18/what-is-fake-news-pizzagate

Convergence

When newspapers operate online there is **convergence**. Not only are newspapers available online, but their content may change in the process. Online newspapers will use the traditional media language of newspapers but also that of television through embedded video, and that of social media through readers' comments. Online versions of newspapers often differ from the print version as they take on more online attributes (such as **clickbait**). The *Mail* online, for example, is much more celebrity and gossip focused than the print newspaper. The *Observer* online recognisably follows the structure of the print edition, but with greater prominence for the lifestyle, food and sport sections that are kept out of the main section of the print newspaper, plus a much higher proportion of photography and headlines to copy on the homepage.

> **Convergence**: the merging of previously separate media forms in one entity – for example, we use smartphones to stream music.
>
> **Clickbait**: the use of sensational headlines or images to attract clickthroughs on a website.

> **Revision activity**
>
> See whether you can find one example of a story from the *Observer* or the *Guardian* that runs through the print edition, the website, the Twitter feed and the Instagram feed. Does this story change with the different versions?

Targeting audiences

Broadsheet or quality newspapers target an upmarket, middle-class audience, whereas tabloid newspapers target a more downmarket, working-class readership. Thus only broadsheet newspapers still have paywalls on their websites.

More men than women read newspapers, with only the *Daily Mail* attracting significantly more female than male readers. Tabloid newspaper readers are more likely to be male. Online newspapers attract an even more male audience than print newspapers.

Print newspaper readers are usually older than the population as a whole.

Observer audiences

Readership surveys show that many more people read the *Observer* than one might expect from the sales figures because:

● more than one person will read each newspaper
● different people buy the print newspaper from one week to the next
● many more people access the *Observer* online.

You do not need to memorise these figures, they are simply to illustrate the importance of the online audience to the newspaper.

Print (Sept/Oct 2017)	
Circulation	177,000
Readers	800,000

Print and online (Sept 2017)	
Daily readership	2.4 million
Weekly readership	6.3 million
Monthly readership	10.5 million

Observer readers

Monthly UK online *Observer* readers are:

● slightly more male (55 per cent) than female (45 per cent) – this male bias is very common in online news content; the print readership is 50–50
● relatively young (one-third 15–34, two-thirds 35 plus)
● upmarket (three-quarters of the online audience are social class ABC1)
● mostly (two-thirds) using mobiles.

You do not need to memorise the facts in brackets.

These readers are sold to advertisers as affluent, arts and culture lovers, food and drink aficionados, and 'progressives' – forward-looking people who are keen to try new things.

The *Guardian/Observer* website had 152 million unique browsers worldwide in May 2017. The *Guardian* online has different editions targeting different worldwide audiences:

● UK
● US
● Australia.

A substantial proportion of the *Guardian/Observer*'s income from contributors in 2017 came from the USA.

Revision activity

Look at the different *Guardian* online editions – British (www.theguardian.com/uk), US (www.theguardian.com/us-news) and Australian (www.theguardian.com/au) – and briefly note any differences in their choice of content.

Targeting audiences: how the different sections of the print *Observer* are reproduced in the online *Observer*

The print *Observer* has sections that are designed to appeal to different types of readers. These are reproduced online, though they are not so clearly separated as they are in the print edition:

- The main section of the print version consists of news and opinion, a mix of the traditional **hard news** traditionally offered by newspapers and opinion pieces that were once the preserve of current affairs magazines. These appeal to the news-hungry reader. The homepage includes these sections at the top of the page, under the headings 'the observer', 'opinion', 'features' and 'letters and editorials', with the 'cartoon' and 'interviews' slightly further down the page.
- The 'New Review' consists of more comedic opinion pieces, interviews and reviews of theatre, dance, music, cinema, architecture, computer games and television listings. These appeal to the culture consumer. The homepage features these towards the bottom of the pages, under 'reviews'.
- The sports section covers primarily male sports, with a bias towards football and rugby union. This appeals to the sports fan and is written in a stereotypically masculine style. The homepage carries a 'sport' section about two-thirds of the way down the page.
- The magazine contains much lifestyle material such as fashion, gardening, interior decor, well-being, and advice on sex and relationships, as well as more serious opinion pieces and interviews. Much but certainly not all of the lifestyle content appears to be targeting women. The homepage spreads this material across several sections: 'regulars', 'food and lifestyle', 'interviews' and some articles in 'features', meaning that lifestyle elements are more prominent on the website than in the print newspaper, though below the news and opinion as the reader scrolls down the page.

> **Hard news**: serious new stories about sometimes difficult topics.

> **Revision activity**
>
> Compare the different sections of the main *Observer* print newspaper and its supplements with the sections on the *Observer* homepage. Are they similar or different?

How to use theory

Uses and Gratifications

The uses and gratifications approach was proposed by Blumler and Katz to explore how audiences use the media to gain pleasure. This approach can be summarised by the following four headings.

1 **Personal identity**
Newspaper readership can still be used as a symbol of one's social identity. The term 'Guardian reader' connotes a certain type of social attitude and the *Observer* similarly reinforces a set of social and political attitudes in its representations. For example, *Observer* readers like to think of themselves as open-minded and this is reflected in the *Observer*'s practice of allowing both sides of an argument equally to be put when the newspaper is clearly on one side of this argument – over the success of President Trump or Brexit, for example. Even if a reader does not always agree with a viewpoint the newspaper puts forward, they may still be agreeing with the values being espoused and thus reinforcing their own values. This may confirm their sense of identity.

2 **Social interaction and integration**
Newspapers offer stories and opinions to readers that may form the basis of conversations with others (though, traditionally, broadsheets offered the opportunity for privacy in crowded social situations with strangers, such as on a train).
Reading news and opinion about society, politics, sport and culture may help audiences feel more strongly that they are members of a common culture.
Reading articles by familiar columnists and responding with tweets, Instagram comments or comments on the website may replace real social interactions for some readers. Some columnists, such as Nick Cohen in the *Observer*, write strongly argued, almost provocative pieces that often encourage such a response.

3 Entertainment

The entertainment function of newspapers may take various forms:

- humour – in punning headlines, in cartoons, or in comedic opinion pieces such as those by David Mitchell in the *Observer*, for example; audience comments on the website are often the funniest part of the paper
- diversion into a celebrity world of 'glamour'; this is especially true of the tabloid press but the quality press increasingly offer this pleasure, particularly in 'softer' sections such as Lifestyle on the website
- human interest stories in which readers are invited to sympathise with the subjects of the article; these are more common in the supplements to quality newspapers and on image-led feeds such as Instagram where even '@guardian' publishes many human interest stories
- games, puzzles, crosswords and the like
- arts and literature sections such as Culture on the website may offer the pleasure of extremely well-written think pieces and reviews.

4 Surveillance

The major use of newspapers is to gain a sense of knowing what is going on in the world. For those who follow a newspaper online, this feeling may be amplified by a sense of getting the news 'as it happens'. This is particularly marked with Twitter feeds such as '@guardian', with new tweets every few minutes giving a sense of constant updating. Newspapers offer a range of information, for example in the *Observer*:

- hard news stories giving a sense of updating on events
- interpretive articles giving deeper understanding of events
- opinion pieces that can demonstrate a range of opinions in play about current affairs
- in-depth interviews with people in the news
- celebrity and entertainment news and gossip
- cultural reviews and discussions
- sports news and opinion
- lifestyle advice and information.

Not only do individual newspapers give information but the role of the industry as a whole is also to reflect a variety of different viewpoints across the range of newspapers.

Active/passive audiences

Traditionally, the audience for a newspaper was primarily **passive** – they could choose which newspapers to buy and could write to the editor but would otherwise have to accept what they were given.

Online newspapers cultivate a far more **active audience**, but still retain the editorial supremacy of the newspaper itself. Thus, the *Observer* website has little or no user-generated content; the audience are limited to responding to the journalists' output, though they can and do debate with one another. The Twitter and Instagram feeds similarly offer content for response, with generally slightly less debate than on the *Observer* website. As neither is moderated, there is much more opportunity for **trolling** on these feeds, but both seem to encourage a shorter audience attention span, which may discourage debate.

Personal identity: how audiences use the media to reinforce their sense of themselves and their values and find role models for how to behave.

Social interaction and integration: how audiences use the media to interact more with one another and to fit into society.

Surveillance: how audiences use the media to gain knowledge about the world.

Passive audience: have to accept what they are given.

Active audience: participate in the media, e.g. by making content.

Trolling: attempting to disturb social media users by posting aggressive contrary arguments, insults and threats.

Now test yourself

1 A newspaper offers soft news aimed at a downmarket audience. Is it 'broadsheet' or 'tabloid'?
2 Explain why there is no regulatory body established by the government – like Ofcom – for newspapers.
3 State two demographics for typical online *Observer* readers (class and gender).
4 State one way that newspaper owners explicitly exercise control over their newspapers.

Answers on p. 134

How to prepare for the exam

Revise your material on:
● industries for print newspapers
● audiences and industries for online newspapers.

Now answer the exam practice question and compare it to the sample answers studied.

Questions 8 and 9

What these questions involve

REVISED

Question 8 is a 5-mark analysis of the use of media language to create meaning in a newspaper extract.

Question 9 is worth 15 marks and will require the student to draw together elements from their full course of study, including different areas of the theoretical framework and media contexts.

Timing

REVISED

Question 8 is a short essay question that should take about five minutes.

Question 9 is an extended essay question that should take about 15 minutes.

What the examiner is looking for

REVISED

Examiners are looking for answers to both questions that show sophisticated, perceptive and accurate analysis that focuses on how the area required – media language or representation – is used in the extract.

Examiners are further looking, in Question 9, for the answer to make judgements and reach conclusions. This may be best done by ending with a paragraph that comes to a conclusion, even though you may have made judgements throughout the answer. You might signal this by starting the paragraph with 'In conclusion ...'. The words 'How far' at the beginning of the question are a further pointer to your need to make judgements.

Exam practice

Question 8

Analyse the use of media language to create meaning in the extract from *the Observer* homepage. [5]

Question 9*

In this question you will be rewarded for drawing together elements from your full course of study, including different areas of the theoretical framework and media contexts.

'The representations featured in the online *Observer* reflect its values and beliefs.' How far do you agree with this statement in relation to the extract from the *Observer* homepage? In your answer you must:

● analyse the representations in the extract with reference to the *Observer's* values and beliefs
● make judgements and draw conclusions about how far you agree with the statement. [15]

The extract for both questions can be found on the OCR website: www.ocr.org.uk/qualifications/gcse-media-studies-j200-from-2017/assessment/

Look for the link to 'Unit J200/02 – Music and News – Insert – Sample Assessment Material'.

* See below.

Extended response questions

The asterisk (★) next to question 9 is to signpost that this is an extended response answer, meaning that you will be marked on the quality of your essay:

● how well you develop a line of reasoning
● how relevant your answer is throughout
● how well you provide evidence for the points you make.

Bullet-pointed questions

The bullet points in Question 9 tell you exactly what the examiners are looking for in your answer – they state everything you need to do to meet the demands of the mark scheme.

'Full course of study' questions

Sometimes Question 9 may start with: 'In this question you will be rewarded for drawing together elements from your full course of study, including different areas of the theoretical frameworks and media contexts.'

You will see this statement once in each exam paper at the beginning of a 15-mark question (so in this paper it could come before Question 5 or Question 9). The statement means you must cover more than one of the four areas of the theoretical framework – media language, representations, industries and audiences – to achieve the top of the highest mark band.

In Question 9 it would mean that you should cover one other area as well as whichever is asked for in the question – media language and/or representation. The two areas do not have to be covered at equal length, just one point from a second area is enough. Look at the following two sample answers.

Example 1

The representations in the online 'Observer' reflect their liberal values. This is because they are owned by the Scott Trust whose job it is to make sure their newspapers are independent and liberal. If an 'Observer' editor took the newspaper in a different direction he or she would be fired.

This section of the answer would count as covering another area – media industries – in a representation essay, meaning that the answer could access the full range of marks.

Example 2

The representations in the online 'Observer' reflect their liberal values. This is because the 'Observer's' target audience is middle-class 'progressives' who read the 'Observer' for its liberal viewpoint.

This section of the answer is covering another area – media audiences – in a representation essay. Again, it would mean the answer could access the full range of marks.

Making judgements and reaching conclusions

If a question asks 'how far' something is true or you agree with a statement, then this should be the focus of your conclusion. In Question 9 you might argue one of the following:
● that the representations **do** reflect the *Observer*'s values and beliefs
● that the representations **do not** reflect the *Observer*'s values and beliefs
● that some representations **do** and some representations **do not** reflect the *Observer*'s values and beliefs.

Examiners will be told to credit any argument that is backed up by analysis of the extract, so there is no 'right answer' to these questions with which you have to agree. However, it would be very difficult to argue that the representations do not fit the *Observer*'s values and beliefs, so agreeing with the statement would be much easier in this case. You should carry out your analysis first, then make your decision later, based on the evidence.

For example,

In conclusion, the representations do reflect the 'Observer's' values and beliefs. There is a lot of representation of women and foreigners and they take care not to be racist. This shows that they are a liberal newspaper.

This does count as a conclusion, but it is rather too definite and not clearly linked to the evidence. You do not always have to come down on one side or the other in a debate – you can argue that both sides are partially correct or that the situation is more nuanced than the question suggests.

Revision activity

How might you improve this conclusion by arguing for and against the idea that the homepage reflects the *Observer's* beliefs and values?

Contexts

One analysis question across the two exam papers will ask you to refer to media contexts in your answer. This might be Question 8 or 9 in this section. If you are analysing an unseen extract, you may be able to apply one of the following contexts:

● **changes in gender roles**
● **changing attitudes to sexualities**
● **multiculturalism**
● **celebrity culture**
● **consumerism**.

> **Changes in gender roles**: the increasing role of women in public life (e.g. politics) following the impact of 1970s feminism.
>
> **Changing attitudes to sexualities**: the increasingly visible role of LGBT people in public life and acceptance of different sexualities.
>
> **Multiculturalism**: the change from a white society in which racism is 'normal' to one characterised by many different racial and ethnic groups.
>
> **Celebrity culture**: the organisation of popular culture around celebrities – people who are famous for being famous.
>
> **Consumerism**: the expectation that people will aspire to 'better themselves' by buying goods and services (e.g. clothes, cars, houses) that mark out their individual identity. (Opposing ideas to consumerism may include: to reject material goods or to follow one's duty to a group or society.)

For these questions you will revise:
● applying media language and representation analysis to products and applying media contexts.

You should revise the audience and industries content covered under Question 7 for any questions asking you to draw together elements from your full course of study.

Media language and the print *Observer*

REVISED

The *Observer* and *Guardian* newspapers changed format in early 2018 from the previous Berliner size (smaller than a broadsheet, bigger than a tabloid) to the current tabloid size and redesigned some aspects of the media language.
● Students sitting the GCSE exam in 2019: you may be given an extract to analyse that might be from the print newspaper. In this case, the newspaper will be in the old, Berliner format as the extract has to be from before September 2017.
● Students sitting the exam from 2020 onwards: if you are asked to analyse an extract from the print newspaper, it will be the new tabloid version. If you are given an extract from the website or Twitter or Instagram feeds to analyse, it will be a version of these from after January 2018.

For media language, you should analyse one or more of the following, including the **connotations** created:
● layout – e.g. any distinctive use of layout, the proportion of space, image and copy, the use of cluttered or ordered layout, the use of symmetrical and **asymmetrical layout**, house style
● typography – e.g. serif and sans serif typefaces, specialist typefaces, bold, italics
● colour – e.g. colour tones, colour saturation, house style
● images – e.g. graphics, camerawork and mise-en-scène in photography, digital manipulation

> **Exam tip**
>
> You do not need to learn or memorise the changes in the design but it can help to be familiar with the media language of the version of the *Observer* that you may be asked to analyse in the exam.

> **Connotations**: additional meanings and associations that can be interpreted from the detailed analysis of media products.
>
> **Asymmetrical layout**: the page is not evenly balanced or centred; such layout is typical as it adds interest.

- use of language – e.g. formal and informal registers, direct mode of address, puns, colloquialisms, slang
- how the media language portrays aspects of reality, presents a point of view and represents the world to create messages and values – e.g. what is celebrated or criticised by the media language
- how the newspaper uses the advantages of print technology – e.g. detailed copy (writing), use of layout to confer significance on articles, large-sized photography
- the **generic conventions** of quality newspapers:
  - traditional **mastheads** in serif fonts
  - smaller proportion of headlines and images to copy (writing) compared with the tabloids
  - serif fonts used for headlines and capitalised as in a sentence
  - formal language register
  - restrained use of colour
- use of **intertextuality** in newspapers – e.g. references to other media products.

> **Generic conventions**: shared elements of a media product, which are repeated so often that they become familiar.
>
> **Masthead/title piece**: the masthead is technically the name of the newspaper on the editorial page, but the term is often used to describe the name of the publication on the front cover, also known as the title piece.
>
> **Intertextuality**: references to other media products that are expected to be recognised by the audience.

Layout in the *Observer* main newspaper (i.e. not the supplements)

Both the tabloid and Berliner formats of the newspaper used a similar layout.

Columns	A five-column layout in most of the newspaper, apart from the 'Comment' section where important articles and the editorial are laid out in four columns.
	Columns are usually right and left aligned (reaching the margins on both the right and left sides) in the news section to create ordered-looking columns. Words are hyphenated and continue on the next line rather than using justification (spreading out the words so they fit the column width). In the 'Focus' and 'Comment' sections the columns are more likely to be left aligned and jagged on the right-hand side, especially for the longer four-column reads, as this helps readers follow the flow of an argument.
	Columns are not broken up by crossheads (a sub-heading that breaks up a long story) as they would be in a tabloid newspaper. They are, however, at times broken up by:
	- a pull quote – a quote in larger font outside the column that highlights an aspect of the article
	- a sidebar – a panel or box containing images and/or extra information
	- drop capitals at the beginning of some paragraphs (e.g. in the 'Comment & Analysis' section) in the tabloid version of the paper only.
	This house style connotes formality, seriousness and detail – that the page is there to deliver lengthy journalism. Occasionally, an image is used that breaks up the strict columns by the text wrapping around the image. This adds a touch of informality.
Headlines	Conventionally used – either as banner headlines spreading over the whole page or the most important headline at the top left.
	Most headlines are followed by a standfirst – a block of text introducing the story. The byline – giving the journalist's name – may be within the standfirst or be located below the standfirst. The front-page lead story will often use bullet points for its standfirst, connoting more urgent, 'punchy' news.
Headers	Each page has a header – a 'folio' – that labels the page, either as part of a section or as a special report on a topic.
Use of images	The proportion of images – photographs and occasional graphics – was seldom as much as half of the page area in the Berliner format. The tabloid version has a slightly higher proportion of photographs on the page. The images are laid out in a formal manner, respecting the copy columns and with a restrained use of overlapping or text wrapping used to give emphasis. This connotes objectivity and 'hard news'.

The front page

The *Observer* front page has a similar layout in both Berliner and tabloid formats:

- At the top of the page are colourful **skyboxes**— an information panel about inside stories that aims to tempt the reader. At times, usually when the *Observer* feels it has to take a strong stand on a news event, this may be replaced or shrunk by a quote from the editorial.
- Under the skyboxes is the masthead 'The Observer', taking up most of the page width – broadsheet newspapers give their mastheads space to 'breathe', to connote the authority of the newspaper.
- There are usually two news articles on the front page so there is rarely a banner headline taking up the whole width of the page; the page usually has an asymmetrical layout with the lead headline on the top left.
- There is usually only one photograph on the front page between about one-quarter to one-third of the size of the combined articles on the page. This is often a **standalone**.
- The Berliner-format front page often carried a banner advertisement at the bottom of the page.

The connotations of the front-page layout are, as for the inside pages, formality, seriousness and detail, but the use of the skyboxes creates more friendly and inviting connotations rather like the cover lines of a magazine.

Typography

Typography differs somewhat in the Berliner and tabloid versions of the newspaper.

The Berliner *Observer* main newspaper

The *Observer* masthead – the words 'The Observer' on the front page – was in a **sans serif font** with rounded ends (the font is called Antenna Condensed Black, but you do not need to memorise this). This was a very 'straightforward' font – it has bold and emphatic connotations – and like all sans serif fonts it connoted modernity. The font fitted the *Observer*'s self-image as a liberal newspaper for 'progressives'.

Headlines were mostly in **serif fonts**, which connoted the formality and seriousness associated with 'quality' newspapers, but the second headline on the front page was often in a less bold sans serif font. Moreover, the standfirsts under the headlines were all in sans serif fonts, as were the pull quotes throughout the paper. This mix of styles was designed to connote, perhaps, a combination of tradition and modernity.

The body copy (the long writing) in the articles was written in a serif font – serif copy fonts are considered easier to read when there is a large amount of text and are traditional in newspapers.

The tabloid *Observer* main newspaper

All fonts are serif in the redesigned *Observer*. The masthead uses a slightly more rounded version of the font used for the *Guardian* masthead, which uses a font designed especially for the newspapers. This font is a mixture of bold and elegantly thin strokes, connoting confidence and elegance. It is used throughout the headlines in the main section of the newspaper, creating a strong sense of house style. The boldest versions of this font are reserved for the masthead and drop capitals, which punctuate the pages and give a strong sense of unity to the design.

Skybox: an information panel about inside stories, above the masthead on the front page of a newspaper, that aims to tempt the reader.

Standalone: a newspaper picture story that can stand on its own or, on the front page, will lead to a story inside the paper.

Revision activity

Investigate the layout of the tabloid version of the *Observer*. Is the house style different in terms of:
- number of columns?
- use of alignment and justification?
- use of headlines and standfirsts?
- use of headers?
- layout of the front page?

Do any changes create different connotations?

Sans serif and serif fonts: serifs are small ornaments in fonts – sans serif fonts don't have serifs, serif fonts do.

The body copy (the long writing) in the articles is written in a serif font – serif copy fonts are considered easier to read when there is a large amount of text and are traditional in newspapers.

Colour

The Berliner *Observer* main newspaper

The *Observer* had a house colour linked to the brand but also used different colours throughout the newspaper to brand different sections:

- the *Observer* brand was linked to the grey-blue colour used for the title piece 'The Observer'
- this colour was used for the 'Comment' section of the newspaper, which included the editorial, with the name again in the masthead – the heart of the paper
- other sections were marked by different colours – light blue for news, brown for 'In Focus', green-blue for 'Business', light blue for 'Travel'. These colours were chosen to contrast with each other rather than for definite connotations.

The tabloid *Observer* main newspaper

Colours are used throughout the main newspaper to brand different sections, but most of the differences in colour are subtle: four different blues differentiate the News, World News, Focus and Travel sections; the only contrasting colours are for the Comment & Analysis and Business & Cash sections with purple-red and orange colours, respectively. Headlines are now primarily in black. The first edition of the tabloid Observer used an aubergine colour in three different elements of the front page, creating a strong splash of colour with sophisticated connotations.

Images

The *Observer* uses full-colour photography throughout the newspaper, bringing colour, visual interest and layout variety to each page. Most images are of politicians, celebrities and 'ordinary people' caught up in news stories. Some photographs are taken as **close-ups** (or cropped to close-ups) but most are more respectful medium and **long shots**, connoting a news orientation rather than a personality orientation.

The weekly cartoon at the centre of the newspaper carries on a long tradition of political cartooning in journalism. These cartoons often have deliberately grotesque connotations.

Use of language

The use of language on the front page of the *Observer* varies to reflect its different functions.

Headlines are written in journalistic style – 'newsy' but using a **formal language register**. Examples include:

- 'Police search Surrey house as teenager held over tube bomb' (17 September 2017) – the language connotes the objective reporting of fact
- 'Furious Tory MPs reject May threats over Brexit votes' (3 September 2017) – the objective reporting of fact is mixed with more emotive language such as 'furious' and 'threats'
- 'May in battle for survival as Tories sharpen knives' (1 October 2017) also uses more colloquial language such as 'sharpen knives'

Close-up: a head-and-shoulders shot or closer.

Long shot: a shot of the whole body or further away.

Formal language register: complex sentences conveying an objective tone.

- 'Spain announces direct rule to crush Catalan "rebellion"' (22 October 2017) uses mostly formal objective language, but the use of speech marks around the word 'rebellion' connotes a disagreement with this version of reality.

The language in the skyboxes at the top of the page is more informal:
- more superlative and enticing, e.g. '25 best beauty buys' (3 September 2017), '20 best seafood recipes' (24 September 2017)
- more comedic, e.g. the punning 'Porn in the USA' (10 September 2017)
- more personal, e.g. 'The George Michael I knew' (15 October 2017)
- more helpful, e.g. 'How to snooze better' (24 September 2017)
- including **direct address**, e.g. 'A guide to the divided parliament deciding your future' (10 September 2017).

> **Direct address:** addressing the reader by using the words 'you' or 'your', for example.

Media language and values

The *Observer*'s mainstream liberal values – a belief in tolerance, fairness and progress – are reflected in the choice of media language, which is itself mainstream but with a modern twist (through, for example, its use of colour and sans serif fonts – Berliner format only).

The media language is designed to connote that the newspaper is packed full of news – a connotation that celebrates the value of information, of knowing and understanding what is happening in the world.

The advantages of print technology

The print version of the newspaper provides much more detail on the front page than the online version does on the homepage – this is because print is a better technology for detailed writing.

A print newspaper allows for much more varied layout than a webpage, as it is less constrained by size considerations.

A print newspaper can print large photographs and graphics, which create more visual variety and interest than on the website, especially if this is viewed on a mobile phone.

Advertisers can be offered a range of display advertising, including full-page adverts, and classified advertising (e.g. in the travel and review sections). The authority of the print newspaper as a brand may transfer to its print advertising.

Generic conventions

The *Observer* follows most of the media language conventions of the quality press:

Convention	Berliner *Observer*	Tabloid *Observer*
Traditional mastheads in serif fonts	No – the masthead/title piece is sans serif	Yes
Smaller proportion of headlines and images to copy (writing) compared with the tabloids	Yes	Yes, but less so than in the Berliner version
Serif fonts used for headlines and capitalised as in a sentence	Yes, but sans serif used for standfirsts	Yes
Formal language register	Yes	Yes
Restrained use of colour	Yes	Yes

Intertextuality

There are many references to other media products in any one issue of the *Observer*:

- references to films, television, radio and recorded music in the 'New Review' supplement
- references to other media products in the news, such as stories about the media, how politicians, creative artists and celebrities use the media, or references to media products to illustrate stories.

News stories are themselves usually intertextual – they reference previous similar stories (e.g. one flood story might trigger other flood stories) or previous versions of the same story (a Sunday paper like the *Observer* will often summarise how a story has developed over the week).

The *Observer* website

REVISED

Media language

Most media language is very similar on the website but some is necessarily different and these differences are discussed below.

Layout

The *Observer* homepage is part of the *Guardian* website – the whole site carries the same layout. Opinion pieces were once collected under the label 'Comment is Free', but now they are simply labelled 'Opinion', in both the *Guardian* and the *Observer*. All these carry a 'Comments' section at the bottom of the page. For example, a big think piece, such as that by Andrew Rawnsley before the 2017 budget, elicited 764 comments in less than a week.

The PC version of the *Observer* website has a four-column layout with generous white margins on either side. These four columns can be clearly seen in the example on the OCR website. The margins can be bought by advertisers, which gives the appearance of 'taking over the homepage'. However, the *Observer* does not usually carry this advertising, instead routinely selling the 'billboard' space above the masthead and **navigation bar**. Display advertising in the body of the page often disturbs the four-column layout, e.g. changing to three columns to fit in the advert, which perhaps draws attention to the advert.

The mobile version has a single-column layout with no margins and no advertising at the head of the page, meaning that the masthead can be read without scrolling, even in landscape format. In this version the adverts are usually given the whole page width and readers must scroll past them.

The layout in both versions is ordered and clean in a similar manner to the print publication. The major difference is the far greater number of stories on the online homepage (compared with a print front page) and the lack of body copy – each story is represented by a headline, sometimes with an image and sometimes with a standfirst. Devices are used to break up the list of headlines: section headings in the left margin (on PCs), variation in the size of the images, and colour blocks. This succession of headlines connotes both choice and plenty – that audiences are given a cornucopia of material they can explore.

Clicking through to a story leads to a page with a different wide single-column layout, headed by a headline and standfirst, usually followed by an image. Articles have links to related stories and advertising in the margins. These pages similarly connote order and seriousness, with lengthy body copy dominating the page.

Typography

The masthead before January 2018 was in the same sans serif font as that used for the print edition, with the same bold, emphatic and modern connotations. In January 2018 the website masthead changed to the same serif typeface black on white design as that used for the tabloid *Guardian* newspaper.

There is some use of sans serif fonts in the header and footer of the webpage – which is conventional for a website as these fonts look clean and modern. However, serif fonts are used almost exclusively throughout the rest of the homepage, carrying connotations of seriousness, authority and objectivity that are appropriate to a quality newspaper, if unusual for a website. Body copy in the articles is in a serif font, as in the print edition.

Colour

The colour palette followed is that of the *Guardian* online house style, not that of the print *Observer*. The masthead before January 2018 was a slab of cool and confident blue as used in the *Guardian* print newspaper. This contrasted with the other house colour, seen prominently in the extract on the OCR website, which was a 'wine-like' purple-pink colour with connotations of sophistication and confidence.

Following the launch as tabloid newspaper in 2018, the website's colour scheme was redesigned. The masthead is black on a pale grey-blue background that is very neutral in effect, allowing the use of colour variation in the navigation bar: red for News; orange for Opinion; blue for Sport; gold for Culture; purple for Lifestyle. These colours are followed through in the various sections of the website. The redesign connotes liveliness and prioritises ease of navigation over the sophistication of a simpler colour scheme.

Images

The website uses photographs similar to those in the print newspaper – nearly all are of people, mostly politicians, creative people, celebrities and sportspeople, but many are more closely cropped than in the print edition. This is perhaps because smaller images require a more definite focus and cannot rely on incidental detail.

How the *Observer* website uses the advantages of online technology

The website publishes comments from readers after articles and on the *Guardian* 'Comment is Free' site. These comments are actively moderated – it is quite common to see that comments have been removed – so the newspaper offers both a safe space for debate and genuine user-generated content as readers engage in active debate with one another.

Hyperlinks on the website enable readers to follow a story in multiple directions, plus suggestions for related articles appear at the side and the bottom of an article to suggest further reading. The website offers a search facility and an archive of old articles.

Now write a full answer to the Example Question 8 on p.106 in five minutes.

Compare your answer to the following sample answer.

> Colour is used to create a house style by means of a limited colour palette – two house colours of royal blue and a wine purple on a white background. This and the use of a dark blue colour for the header connotes serious, sober, objective news. The use of a serif typeface for the headings, the highly ordered layout of the homepage, the fairly limited use of photographs and graphics to minimise visual clutter similarly connotes formality and objectivity.
>
> On the other hand, the use of a bold, sans serif, white on blue mostly lower case font for the masthead connotes a modern and confident paper. This fits the Observer brand and 'progressive' values.
>
> The language use includes both personal (e.g. 'Can I forgive', 'My lifelong affair...') and third person statements (e.g. 'Murray too good for Verdasco in Dubai') but creates an overall objective mode of address.

Exam tip

This version of the website is no longer available, following the redesign that launched in January 2018, so you will not be expected to be familiar with this design.

This answer would gain a Level 3 mark (4–5 marks) because it is a:
- sophisticated analysis of how media language is used in at least two examples from the extract
- highly relevant response to the question, demonstrated by full focus on how media language is used in the extract to create meaning.

It would probably gain full marks because it meets all the marking criteria fully (even though it is not a perfect answer).

Revision activity

Analyse *The Observer* homepage and at least one article and note any changes to the media language described above.

Media language and the *Guardian's* Twitter feed

REVISED

Content from the *Observer* newspaper is branded as *Guardian* content on Twitter, so any *Observer* content you would be asked to analyse will come from the *Guardian's* Twitter feed '@guardian'. Most of the media language on the page is determined by Twitter, but there are some elements chosen by the *Guardian*:

- the header before January 2018 used a photograph of corals growing underwater, a photo whose colour palette of blue and white fitted that of the *Guardian* house colours; the header after the redesign in January 2018 consisted of the black on white masthead with a series of colour bars reproducing the colour scheme of the newspaper website
- the logo next to each tweet – before January 2018, a white lower-case 'g' in a blue circle; after then, an upper-case white on black 'G'
- the house colour for links – blue

Exam tip

You do not need to learn or memorise the changes in the *Observer* social media feeds or the website. If you are asked to analyse one of these you will be given an extract to work from.

- the branding of images linking to stories – before January 2018, a blue footer including 'theguardian' in light and darker blue; after then, the white on black logo (except for Opinion pieces, which use the *Guardian* Opinion orange branding).

These all confirm the *Guardian* brand identity, suggesting connotations of coolness and sophistication within the constraints of the Twitter 'look'.

How the *Guardian* Twitter feed uses the advantages of online technology

The Twitter feed is updated regularly – it is used primarily to display the images and headlines from the latest stories – and so embraces the instantaneous and immediate nature of online communication.

Comments from audience members are published on the site and readers engage in active debate with one another, though curtailed in part by the Twitter word limit. Many readers retweet or 'like' posts.

Revision activity

Access the *Guardian* Twitter feed and note which tweets receive the most 'likes' and 'retweets'.

Media language and the *Guardian*'s Instagram feed

REVISED

Content from the *Observer* newspaper is branded as *Guardian* content on Instagram, so any *Observer* content you would be asked to analyse will come from the *Guardian*'s Instagram feed '@guardian'. Instagram offers fewer opportunities for branding by use of media language than Twitter. The only significant differences in the look of the *Guardian* feed from that of the *Sun* feed, for example, are:
- the different logos (white on red for the *Sun*, white on blue before January 2018 for the *Guardian*, white on black after)
- differences in the photographs and captions.

The Instagram feed, being image driven, appears to cover more 'soft' news stories than the website or Twitter feed. The captions suggest that the hard stories that are covered are being explained in relatively simple language to an audience that is not expected to be up to date with UK news and current affairs. Thus the language is slightly less formal, sometimes using direct address and other more conversational techniques.

Revision activity

Access the *Guardian* Instagram feed and note which five photographs and/or videos receive the most 'likes'. Note why you think these are so popular.

Representations in the *Observer*

REVISED

Representations do not change dramatically from one version of the newspaper to another – the print edition, the website, the Twitter and Instagram feeds all tend to convey the same view of the world and liberal values. We will explore how representations reflect these core values and world-view across the forms first, then consider whether there are any differences between the different forms.

For representations, you should analyse:
- how the producers have chosen to construct a version of reality that represents events, social groups and ideas to fit their purposes
- the viewpoints, messages, beliefs and values conveyed

- how and why **stereotypes** have been used (e.g. to enable quick interpretation by audiences)
- how and why social groups are under-represented or misrepresented
- the social, cultural and political significance of the themes and issues addressed
- how representations reflect their social/cultural, political and historical contexts.

> **Stereotype**: an over-simplified portrayal of a member of a social group, place, event or issue, which is based on assumptions and judgements about them.

The *Observer* version of reality and the Scott Trust values

REVISED

The Scott Trust, which owns the *Observer*, exists to ensure its newspapers are independent and carry on a 'liberal tradition'. The liberal tradition includes beliefs:
- in the rights of the individual (e.g. human rights)
- that all individuals are of equal worth (e.g. democracy)
- that all peoples of the world are of equal worth (internationalism)
- in progress (in society, in science and technology).

Acting within this liberal tradition, we would expect the representations in the *Observer* newspaper to:
- promote democracy and human rights, particularly to protect the individual against the power of the state or other powerful institutions such as 'big business'
- celebrate individuality, diversity, tolerance and allowing opposing points of view
- care for people no matter where in the world they live (internationalism)
- seek solutions to pressing social problems
- be open-minded about change.

In terms of politics, liberals support parties of the centre. People who consider themselves 'liberals' are a wider group than the members of the Liberal Democrat party; they include the more central wings of both the Conservative Party and the Labour Party. They criticise:
- 'extreme' right-wing authoritarian ideas that limit freedom for some groups
- 'extreme' left-wing ideas that limit the freedom of the individual.

The *Observer* and the *Guardian* do not support any one political party. It is a key feature of the newspapers that different writers express different political views, though only a few of the writers support the Conservative Party. They have recommended readers to vote for different parties at different elections, usually either the Labour Party or the Liberal Democrats. They are usually critical of many Conservative Party policies.

Liberal values and news stories

REVISED

Let's take the two front-page stories in the print *Observer* for 19 November 2017 as an example.

Lead story

'Joyous crowd throng Harare as Mugabe era nears the end' (Harare is the capital of Zimbabwe, a country that had suffered violence under the dictatorial rule of Robert Mugabe.)

This story fits liberal values in the following ways:

- an international story makes the main headline (values internationalism)
- the story is about celebrating the fall of a dictator (values democracy and freedom)
- the front-page photograph of a smiling African woman wearing a '#StepDown' beret (values diversity in representation with an **anti-stereotype** of an African woman who is not sexually objectified as a woman or seen as an object of study or concern as an African).

Second story

'A thousand nurseries shut as childcare crisis mounts.' This story fits liberal values in the following ways:

- it is about a pressing social problem – the funding crisis in children's nursery provision
- it is critical of Conservative government policies to fund childcare.

Stereotypes, under-representation and misrepresentation

The liberal values of the *Observer* newspaper mean that it should celebrate the worth of every individual, regardless of social background, so we should expect the newspaper to make a special effort to:

- avoid stereotyping, looking instead to promote anti-stereotypes
- avoid misrepresentation
- represent groups that are otherwise under-represented.

All of these are difficult:

- Stereotypes are perpetuated because they are a simple and quick way to communicate as they may be based in factual reality (such as differences in power) and because it is not always easy to spot your own use of stereotypes.
- Groups may be inadvertently misrepresented or under-represented because few or none of the media producers belong to that group – for example, poorly educated people are much less likely to become journalists.
- The **ideologies** that govern our society will underpin all the assumptions we make about people – we will not notice when we all make the same assumptions, only when those assumptions are challenged (e.g. when Western feminism is attacked by those who believe women are inferior).

Stereotyping and news stories

Newspaper headlines are a good place to look for stereotypes as they have to be quickly and easily understood. The two headlines we looked at previously both rely on stereotypes to ensure instant recognition. Whether or not these stereotypes are 'true' they are still stereotypes – a simplified judgement:

- The headline 'Joyous crowd throng Harare as Mugabe era nears the end' uses a long-established stereotype that Mugabe was a bad ruler.
- The headline 'A thousand nurseries shut as childcare crisis mounts' uses the stereotype that it is good for children to be given well-funded care and that it is a bad thing for a government to under-fund childcare.

Both these headlines use stereotypes widely held by Western liberals who make up the producers and audiences for this newspaper.

Let's look at the representations in the extract from the online *Observer* on the OCR website: www.ocr.org.uk/qualifications/gcse-media-studies-j200-from-2017/assessment/ (click on 'Unit J200/01 Music and news – insert – sample assessment material').

The 'features' section uses stereotypes but also undermines them at times.

Some articles are clearly stereotypical:
● 'In search of chic: fashion shopping in Paris' relies on a stereotype of Paris that is so strong it may be called a 'myth' – Paris as chic and fashionable (this perhaps under-represents ugly and unstylish Paris).
● The image standing in for 'Stranded refugees' – a silhouetted figure holding a barbed wire fence – is instantly recognisable as it fits the liberal stereotype of maltreated refugees (this perhaps under-represents successful refugees).

Some articles use stereotypes in an ambiguous way:
● 'Gigi Hadid: A model with a fabulous figure (30m Instagram followers)' deliberately uses the stereotype of the objectified woman ('a fabulous figure') then undermines it by confounding the readers' stereotypical expectations of models.

Some use anti-stereotypes:
● 'Get out: Jordan Peele on making a hit comedy-horror movie out of America's racial tensions' presents an anti-stereotype in showing an image of a black American film director (however, linking his film to representation of race then perhaps reinforces the stereotype of film directors being white males by placing him as an exception who deals with race issues).

The 'sport' section appears heavily gender stereotypical in that only sportsmen are featured in the photographs and only one sportswoman is named in the section, reinforcing the stereotypical equation of masculinity and sport.

The 'interview' section also appears heavily stereotypical as the writer is female, the photographer male, the dancer (pictured in the dance studio) female, the sculptor (pictured in front of sculptures) male, it is a man interested in science, and all the interviewees are white. However, the dancer explicitly questions gender stereotyping in dance.

The 'food and lifestyle' section includes an image of a stereotypical event – the family dinner – captured in the overhead angle of a set of arms clinking glasses and the caption about a 'family gathering'.

Under-representation is easier to analyse than misrepresentation. For example, you can count the number of images of men and women in the extract and note that there are 17 men in the photographs and only five women – this is evidence of under-representation. However, to prove misrepresentation entails showing that the reality is different to the media representation, which can't be done in a Media Studies analysis.

You can, however, analyse how far the representations are **diverse** – more diverse representations are less likely to misrepresent as there should be less stereotyping. In some newspapers – such as certain tabloids where most of the women featured are stereotypically young, thin and wearing bikinis – it is clearly possible to demonstrate misrepresentation.

In the *Observer* extract you could note that the women in the photographs are a rape victim, model, mother, writer and dancer, whereas men are represented as a rapist, film director, father, musicians, boxer, photographer, cyclists, tennis star, rugby players, photographer and sculptor. This suggests more diverse images of masculinity and less diverse representations of femininity.

It may be that under-representation always contributes to misrepresentation because fewer representations mean more stereotyping and because under-represented groups often don't work in the media so nobody notices the misrepresentation.

Revision activity

Analyse a number of headlines and images on the website in terms of their use of stereotypes.

Social, cultural and political significance of themes and issues

The *Observer* covered the following issues in the 12 front-page leads between 3 September and 19 November 2017:

Issue	Number of lead stories
British politics	8
International politics (Africa)	1
Mental health care	1
Terrorism	1
Welfare cuts	1

Thus, the number one theme in the front-page news is 'government' – how and by whom the country is run. This is to be expected of the quality press, which see themselves as democracy's watchdog, constantly on alert for danger and misbehaviour. This is the political context in which press freedom applies – the press have a role in informing the public as only an informed public can make properly democratic decisions.

How representations reflect contexts

Social/cultural, political and historical contexts will be covered under Question 10, where the influence of contexts today will be compared with the influence of contexts in the 1960s.

Now test yourself

TESTED

1 Is the font for the masthead on the *Observer* serif or sans serif?
2 List five generic conventions of quality newspapers.
3 What is unusual about the *Guardian/Observer*'s use of fonts on the website?
4 Are photographs on the website more closely cropped or less closely cropped compared with those in the print edition?
5 How is the *Guardian* Instagram content different to the newspaper print and web editions?
6 Given the *Observer*'s liberal values, what would it support?
7 Why might under-representation lead to misrepresentation?

Answers on p. 134

How to prepare for the exam

Practise analysing the media language and representations in:
● the print *Observer*
● the *Observer* homepage and opinion pieces on the website that attract comments
● the *Guardian* Twitter feed
● the *Guardian* Instagram feed.

Now write a full answer to the Example Question 9 on p.106 in 15 minutes.

Compare your answer to the following sample answer.

Many representations in the 'features' section convey the newspaper's actively socially liberal viewpoint. For example, its internationalism is evident in its representation of India, America and the sympathetic representation of the plight of refugees in the features section. The article on possibly forgiving a serious criminal offence values tolerance and understanding rather than a crackdown on crime and criminals.

The influence and embrace of multiculturalism is reflected in the routinely ethnically mixed photographic representations and the anti-stereotypical representation of a black film director.

Similarly, though the sport coverage is still mostly male, there is an attempt at a gender balance through the rest of the content.

Many representations convey the newspaper's (liberal) feminist viewpoint, e.g. the joke about the model's 'fabulous' Instagram figure undermines common gender stereotypes by drawing attention to them and this is combined with an image that does not sexually objectify the woman; the reporting of Julie Cunningham's foregrounding of gender inequality in performance presents her feminist analysis as righteous anger.

The representations in the Interviews section convey a valuing of the arts and science, reflecting the Observer's liberal belief in progress, as well as its well-educated audience.

On the other hand, the male bias in the Sports section does not fit the Observer's liberal feminist values. Only one female sportsperson is mentioned and none is photographed – all the photographs represent traditional masculinity, as does some of the aggressive language. The whole sports section could be from any newspaper.

In terms of audiences, the food and lifestyle section reflects the Observer's affluent middle-class readership and the social context of consumerism rather more than its liberal values by representing dining out at expensive restaurants and choosing wines for family gatherings. This is again reflected in the representation of expensive leisure activities such as shopping in Paris for 'chic'. These could all be from any quality newspaper with a middle-class audience. Such content will attract advertising as it offers an appropriate environment and an audience to sell to advertisers as active and affluent consumers.

In terms of media industries, the content reflects a trend in journalism towards softer news and features that are cheaper to supply due to competition and declining newspaper income, e.g. interviews with people who are seeking publicity and coverage of regular events such as sport.

In conclusion, the representations in the online Observer partially reflect their values and partially reflect what a quality newspaper must do to appeal to a middle-class audience, with a range of interests, and the advertisers. However, the absence of obvious 'clickbait' in the extract reflects how the Observer is partly protected from economic pressures by its ownership model and can offer serious journalism.

This answer would gain a Level 3 mark (11–15 marks) because:
- it is a sophisticated relevant and accurate analysis of relevant aspects of the extract supported by a range of examples
- it draws together knowledge and understanding from the full course of study – representations, audience, industries and contexts
- a clear judgement and conclusion is reached and is fully supported by the analysis.

It would probably gain full marks because it meets all the marking criteria fully (even though it is not a perfect answer).

Question 10

What this question involves

REVISED ☐

This is a 10-mark knowledge and understanding question about the influence of media contexts on print newspapers. This will refer to one of the following options:
- historical newspapers from the 1960s
- contemporary newspapers produced during your course of study
- both historical and contemporary newspapers.

Timing

REVISED ☐

This is a short essay question that should take about ten minutes.

What the examiner is looking for

REVISED ☐

Examiners are looking for understanding of how media contexts influence newspapers, with examples from the set newspapers you have studied.

For this question you will revise:
- how media contexts influence newspapers
- how the three set historical *Observer* front pages from the 1960s reflect their contexts
- how the two contemporary *Observer* front pages you have studied reflect their contexts.

Exam practice

Question 10

Explain how broadsheet newspapers reflect the historical contexts in which they were produced. Refer to stories from the set *Observer* front pages from the 1960s that you have studied to support your answer.

In your answer you must refer to relevant media contexts.

[10]

How media contexts influence newspapers

Contexts can influence newspapers in a number of ways.

- The social make-up of newspaper producers and audiences: this will be affected by social and cultural change. For example, in the 1960s most producers and readers were white males, whereas today there will be more women and ethnic minority producers and audiences. LGBT producers in the 1960s would not go public about their illegal sexuality (for men) and LGBT audiences would not expect to be served by the mainstream media.
- The events and issues available to be reported in newspapers:
  - Newspapers in Britain did not report so much on female or ethnic minority political leaders as there were so few. LGBT stories were very limited by the closeted lifestyle adopted by the communities.
  - Celebrity culture did exist but was less developed than today, so quality newspapers carried more hard news and less about celebrities.
  - Consumerism was developing in the 1960s but less so than today, so today's newspapers will carry more lifestyle content and marketing than their 1960s counterparts.
  - Social change was a major issue in 1960s Britain, where a younger generation were demanding new freedoms, often resisted by some of the older generation who decried 1960s 'permissiveness': legalising homosexuality, making divorce and contraception available, making abortion legal, and allowing more sexual and satirical content on the mass media. These social issues drove newspaper stories.
- The political role of newspapers: newspapers in the 1960s were key political opinion-formers as the other media did not carry as much political content as they do today (no 24-hour rolling news channels) and the online media did not exist. Even the popular press in the mid-1960s carried much more political news than today – the tabloid revolution that created the sensationalist popular press we have today launched slightly later.

How the three set historical *Observer* front pages from the 1960s reflect their contexts

You have been given three front pages as set products. Note that these are from the same historical period as the historical television programme, *The Avengers*, you studied for Paper 1 Section A. Note that you do not need to remember from which front page each story comes, nor the dates of each of the front pages, just the ways in which the stories and layout of the front pages reflect their contexts.

Many news stories from the 1960s front pages of the *Observer* clearly reflect the historical contexts of the time:

- 'Lawyers will urge divorce by consent' – this is an example of the **social/cultural** and **political** context of the 1960s reforms, which included some limited moves to greater gender equality in a patriarchal society; the Law Commission (staffed only by men) is recommending 'divorce by consent' – a change that made it much easier for people to get divorced, an opportunity taken mostly by women leaving their husbands.
- 'Wilson–Brown market clash' – this reflects the **political** context that relations with Europe were as contentious in the 1960s as they are today – Prime Minister Harold Wilson clashes with one of his ministers over joining the Common Market (the forerunner of the EU).

Figure 1.2 The *Observer* 6 Nov. 1966 front page

Figure 1.3 The *Observer* 30 Oct. 1966 front page

Figure 1.4 The *Observer* 20 Oct. 1968 front page

- 'So polite, this North Sea Spy Game', 'Yard suspects Blake used two-way radio', 'America accused of spy frame-up' – these three stories reflect the prevalence of spying news stories in the 1960s Cold War **historical** context. The communist East spied on the capitalist West and vice versa.

- The Cold War also took the form of 'proxy wars' – conflict in third countries, such as Vietnam. Hence, 'Hopes rise for cease-fire in Vietnam' and, indirectly, 'Police will appease marchers', which also reflects the **social/cultural** and **political** context rise of student protest in the 1960s, including 'militant Marxists' opposed to the Vietnam War.

- 'Jackie: we're very happy' reflects a patriarchal **social/cultural** context in which women are most often defined in terms of their relationship with men – here the wife of the dead US president makes a controversial second marriage. The front pages all under-represent women, e.g. one front page has only one reference to women – a photograph of a woman illustrating an article about knitted fashion.

- 'Unions postpone strike' illustrates the high level of strike coverage in the 1960s, reflecting the **political** context of greater union power in that decade. Barbara Castle is mentioned – the only female politician on all three front pages – as trying to argue for less unequal pay for men and women. This reflects the patriarchal **social/cultural** context of the 1960s in which it was accepted that women were paid less than men for doing the same job.

- 'Briton shoots a gold' mentions the 'Black Power' protest at the 1968 Mexico Olympics, reflecting the **social/cultural** context of the success of anti-racist movements in the 1960s; note the unselfconscious use of the term 'Negro', a term that newspapers would not use today due to its racist connotations, showing that even liberals in the 1960s were not so aware of such connotations as we are today in a more explicitly multicultural society.
- 'Stephen Pollock ... with Elizabeth Vambe, 21, a Rhodesian-born African, after their marriage yesterday' reflects the **social/cultural** context of a white culture that saw what were then known as 'mixed marriages' as so unusual as to be newsworthy.

The media language of the front pages also reflects their contexts:

- There is little self-promotion and many more news stories on the front page – this reflects a **social/cultural** context in which consumerism and marketing were less developed than they are today.
- The poor-quality printing and black-and-white photography reflect an era before digital technology.
- The more formal language, e.g. referring to politicians as 'Mr Wilson', reflects the **social/cultural** context of a more deferential society in which people 'knew their place' and looked up to their 'betters'.

Contemporary front pages will reflect changed contexts:

Changed contemporary social/ cultural and political contexts	Examples
The impact of feminism	Reference to female leaders, including political leaders
The impact of multiculturalism	Reference without comment to diverse people defined by race and ethnicity and religion
Changing attitudes to sexuality	'Out' gay people and transgender people in the news, including politicians
Dominance of consumerism and marketing	Self-promotion on front pages; news about brands; the politics of pleasing the voters
Rise of celebrity culture	The personalisation of politics, news about celebrities who are 'famous for being famous'

Revision activity

Analyse the two (or more) contemporary *Observer* front pages you have studied for evidence of the influence of any of the above contexts.

Look for stories in the newspaper that fit these contexts.

Re-read Example Question 10 (p.122) and then the sample answer and the assessment comment below.

There are a number of ways in which newspapers reflect their historical contexts, in the ways these contexts influence their producers, their audiences and the world that they represent through their news stories. For example, Britain was a more patriarchal society in the 1960s compared to today and this meant that most journalists were men, that audiences expected patriarchal representations, and the mostly political news that featured on the front pages was about powerful political figures – nearly all men. Only one female politician – Mrs Castle – features in the three front pages we have studied and even she was unsure about the possibility of achieving equal pay for women, showing the patriarchal assumptions of 1960s Britain. These are further shown by a long article headlined 'Jackie: we're very happy'. The woman in question is of interest only in terms of whom she marries.

Britain was becoming a multicultural society in the 1960s but still saw itself as white, and race relations as a 'problem'. One story about a 'mixed marriage' between a white man and a black woman made the front page as it was considered so unusual in the 1960s. Another story about the Olympic Games – 'Briton shoots a gold' – mentions the Black Power salute made by some athletes, showing the influence of the American Civil Rights movement. The newspaper is trying to be liberal on 'race issues' but still presents a very white point of view.

Other contexts are not obvious because representations are absent – there is no mention of explicitly LGBT people in any stories, as these communities were very closeted before gay liberation in the 1970s. There is also much less marketing and little news about celebrities compared to today, showing less development of celebrity culture and consumerism in the 1960s.

The Cold War is reflected in articles about Russian spy planes ('So polite, this North Sea Spy Game') Russian spies and the Vietnam War. This shows the importance of this historical conflict at the time.

This answer demonstrates clear knowledge of a number of historical contexts and understanding of their influence on the newspaper front pages, which places it firmly in Level 3, probably earning full marks.

Time yourself to see if you can produce a better answer in minutes.

Now test yourself   TESTED ☐

1 Identify one story from the 1960s newspapers that reflects the patriarchal culture that existed before the impact of feminism from the 1970s onwards.
2 Identify one story from the 1960s newspapers that reflects that 1960s Britain saw itself as white rather than multicultural and that race was a 'problem'.
3 Identify one story from the 1960s newspapers that reflects Cold War fear of spies.
4 Identify one story from the 1960s newspapers that reflects Britain's concerns over the relationship with Europe.

Answers on p. 134

How to prepare for the exam

- You need to revise how contexts can influence newspapers.
- You need to be familiar enough with the relevant articles in the three historical newspapers and the two contemporary newspapers you have studied to be able to use them as examples in the exam. Knowing the headlines may help in referring to them, but you don't have to know these as the exam is not a memory test.

► Creating media

As part of your GCSE Media Studies course, you must complete a media production in response to one of four set briefs. Your production, together with your Statement of Intent, will count for 30 per cent of your final grade. Your work will be marked by your teacher and then moderated by an external moderator.

The checklists below are to help you to see whether you need to make any changes to your production or to your Statement of Intent before you submit them.

What are your teacher and the moderator looking for?

REVISED

Your teacher and the external moderator will look carefully to see that you have fulfilled the requirements of the brief, so it is important to check that you have covered all the details in your production. They will also be looking at your Statement of Intent to see how well you have fulfilled your intentions. The details below are taken from the assessment criteria and the indicative content.

First, a reminder that your marks for this component will depend on:
● how well you have used media language to communicate meaning
● how well you have constructed representations as identified in your Statement of Intent
● how well you have targeted your intended audience.

Now use the appropriate checklist below for your Creating Media production.

Note: The point on your use of original material is very important – if you overuse found material, you cannot gain more than 18 marks out of 30 for your production. If you use no original footage, images or text, you cannot gain more than 12 marks out of 30 for your production.

Brief 1: Magazine	Done	Needs improvement
I have produced three pages for my magazine, including a cover and a double-page spread article		
I have used five original images: an original masthead/title, original main cover image and at least two other original images on the front cover and at least two other original images in the double-page spread article		
I have addressed my specific target audience as detailed in the brief of *either* 10–13 year olds *or* 14–18 year olds		
I have used appropriate codes and conventions for the genre		
The title of my magazine is appropriate for my target audience		
I have used typography to give my magazine a consistent house style		
I have used appropriate layout and page design with graphics		
I have used appropriate language, tone, mode of address		
I have used appropriate mise-en-scène in my original photographs		
My magazine has a clear brand identity		
The magazine is my own individual work and I have recorded the use of any unassessed learners on the cover sheet		
I have constructed a particular representation, as outlined in my Statement of Intent		

Brief 2: Television	Done	Needs improvement
My television programme lasts approximately two minutes		
The title of my television programme is appropriate for my target audience		
I have addressed my specific target audience as detailed in the brief of *either* 10–13 year olds *or* 14–18 year olds		
I have used appropriate codes and conventions for the genre		
I have used no more than 20 seconds of found footage		
I have used an appropriate and clear narrative		
I have used mise-en-scène appropriately		
I have used a variety of shots appropriate to the genre		
I have used an appropriate pace of continuity editing		
I have used an appropriate soundtrack		
I planned and edited the production individually and have recorded the use of any unassessed learners on the cover sheet		
I have constructed a particular representation, as outlined in my Statement of Intent		

Brief 3: Music video	Done	Needs improvement
My music video lasts approximately two minutes		
I have addressed my specific target audience as detailed in the brief of *either* 10–13 year olds *or* 14–18 year olds		
I have used appropriate codes and conventions for the genre		
I have used no more than 20 seconds of found footage		
I have used an appropriate and clear narrative		
I have used mise-en-scène appropriately		
I have used a variety of shots appropriate to the genre of music		
I have used appropriate pace and editing devices for the genre of music		
I planned and edited the production individually and have recorded the use of any unassessed learners on the cover sheet		
I have constructed a particular representation, as outlined in my Statement of Intent		

Brief 4: Social, online and participatory	Done	Needs improvement
I have produced two pages for my website, including the homepage and 45 seconds of embedded video or audio material		
I have included three original images, with one working link		
I have addressed my specific target audience as detailed in the brief of *either* 10–13 year olds *or* 14–18 year olds		
I have used appropriate codes and conventions for the genre		
I have used appropriate typography with a consistent house style		
I have used an appropriate layout and page design, with menu, navigation bar, links, logos, graphics		
I have used appropriate language, tone and mode of address		
My website has a clear brand identity		
My website offers opportunities for audience interactivity and user-generated content		
I planned and edited the production and have recorded the use of any unassessed learners on the cover sheet		
I have constructed a particular representation, as outlined in my Statement of Intent		

Statement of Intent

This section is intended to remind you of the purpose of the Statement of Intent and to help you check that you have included all the necessary areas. Remember that it will be assessed alongside your production. If you do not submit the statement, you cannot gain more than 18 marks out of 30 for your production.

Look through your Statement of Intent, making sure that you have covered all the areas below.

	Yes	Needs improvement
My statement is 250–300 words		
I have included details of my chosen brief		
My intended audience (exactly as stated on the brief)		
How I intend to identify, reach and address my target audience		
How I have responded to my research findings – mention some of the following: demographics, psychographics, lifestyle, interests and other media products likely to be consumed by my target audience		
How I will communicate meaning and target my intended audience through generic codes and conventions		
How I will communicate meaning and target my intended audience through my use of media language, e.g. camerawork, use of sound, typography, page design		
How I intend to use stereotypes and/or anti-stereotypes and/or under-represented groups and/or misrepresented groups		
How I will use casting, locations, props, codes of dress, etc. to construct representation		
How I will use narrative structure, e.g. opening, enigma, quest, closure (if appropriate) to construct representation and to target my audience		
How and why I will use intertextuality to target my intended audience (possible reasons are for humour, nostalgia, familiarity or satire)		
My production matches my Statement of Intent		

Now test yourself answers

Paper 1 – Section A: Television and promoting media

Question 1
1 Low-key lighting.
2 High angle.
3 Cross-cutting.

Question 2
1 Panning.
2 Over-simplified portrayal of a person, group, place or event, which is based on assumptions.
3 Shot/reverse shot.

Question 3
1 Personal identity, social interaction and integration, entertainment or surveillance.
2 The 'scheduling' of the programme.
3 BBC One, Wednesday, 8pm.

Question 4
1 a, c, e, f.
2 Personal identity; social interaction and integration; entertainment; surveillance.
3 BARB – the Broadcasters' Audience Research Board.
4 A specialist audience with particular interests, such as online-only channel BBC Three for 16–30 year olds.
5 Ofcom.
6 The licence fee.
7 Television set, DVR box, smartphone, tablet, laptop, games console.
8 Second screening and interactivity (voting for a favourite contestant).

Question 5
1 Anxieties about the threat of a third world war, invasion (Warsaw Pact against NATO) and espionage are all reflected in the episode.
2 Spying was in the news; British double agents had been tried or defected to the Soviet Union; spying was part of the conflict during the Cold War.
3 Someone who tries to undermine a country from within to prepare for an enemy invasion.

4 1970.
5 Steed was in the RAF and then the British intelligence service.
6 M(an) Appeal.
7 He discovers Piggy's gravestone in the deserted airfield.
8 This described the differences in attitudes, values and interests in culture between the older generation and the younger generation in the 1960s.
9 To clarify and combine gender, race, disability and sexuality anti-discrimination Acts.
10 Patriarchal, authoritative, dominant.
11 Stereotypical.
12 Jake Vickers and Donna Prager.
13 DS Jo Moffat giving orders for the police raid reflects the growing number of women in powerful, professional roles. (Or any other similar example.)
14 Ryan is able to show his 'feminine' side when caring for his children, but he is still respected for his stereotypically 'masculine' qualities: bravery, toughness, physical and mental strength, reflecting diverse types of masculinity in 2015. (Or any other similar example.)
15 Ryan is punched during the nudist beach conflict, reflecting the public's lack of respect for the police in 2015 and showing the audience that the police are not as appreciated as they should be. (Or any other similar example.)

Paper 1 – Section B: Promoting Media

Question 6
1 The BBFC.
2 Exhibition.
3 Marketing a media product to an audience.
4 TT Fusion.
5 A global media company, often working in different media sectors.
6 A tent-pole production.
7 Because the film inspired the release of several other linked products, such as *The Lego Movie* video game and other merchandise.

Question 7

1 A tent-pole film is expected to make large profits in order to support the funding of other projects.

2 Because different media sectors worked together on the production of the film. For example, it features characters such as Batman and Superman from other media texts and the film has also been used to inspire the release of a video game.

3 The ensemble cast of the film allows the production to make more money. This is because it can appeal to wider audiences, such as fans of Lego and Batman, which will generate more profit.

4 If the game is released on a variety of platforms, it means more people can play it. This can help to generate more profit.

5 Because many people nowadays have busy lifestyles, so a mobile platform allows them to play video games on the move.

Question 8

1 Answers could include age, gender, ethnicity, profession, income, religion.

2 So that they can be sure an audience will like the product and make changes if necessary.

3 The best promotional campaigns use a variety of promotional strategies in order to reach a variety of audiences. This ensures that as many people as possible are aware of the product and could lead to greater profit.

Question 9

1 The way a media product mixes conventions of different genres.

2 Examples could include heroic protagonist of Emmet, villainous antagonist of President Business, Emmet is on a quest or mission during the narrative, chase scenes, weaponry, an urban, city setting.

3 A widely held but oversimplified belief or idea about a person or group of people.

4 Gender equality.

5 He is represented as a wise old man who is crucial to the narrative as he provides advice and wisdom. This challenges the stereotypical media representation of the older generation as vulnerable, grumpy and lacking in ability to contribute to society.

Paper 2 – Section A: Music

Question 1

1 Bauer publishing.

2 Ofcom.

3 Diversification.

4 Conglomerate.

Questions 2 and 3

1 BBC Radio 2, BBC Radio 4.

2 BBC Radio 1Xtra, BBC Asian Network, BBC Radio 3, any local radio station.

3 By playing distinctive content – live music in performance – which may be too expensive for commercial radio; by targeting an audience not otherwise served by BBC Radio – 16–29 year olds – thus serving the whole population of the UK.

4 Convergence.

5 Radio 1, BBC Four, BBC iPlayer, YouTube.

6 By being distinctive, so offering a sense of personal identity to its loyal audience; by offering a substitute for companionship to isolated audiences, or by offering unusual content that forms the basis of real-life conversation; by offering entertainment, e.g. through the quality of an original performance; by offering a sense of surveillance by giving information, e.g. about bands.

7 Performance to camera, fast-paced editing, use of setting or location to express meaning.

8 Performance and narrative video.

9 Hybridity.

10 To convey the meaning of the song; to promote the artist online and on music television; to promote social messages that reflect well on the artist; to promote the producer (e.g. as a means of launching a career as a film director).

11 Fans of particular artists gain a sense of belonging to a group; audience members can develop a sense of a desired 'outsider' identity by rejecting mainstream pop music; particular pop songs may 'speak' to audience members at times of heightened emotion.

12 The top magazines are owned by international publishers, all based in the USA or Germany.

13 It owns radio and television stations as well as magazines in order to spread the risk associated with the magazine business.

14 Cover price, advertising, sponsored content, product placement, associated activities such as events.

15 They offer a quality 'lean back moment', they have aspirational content, they carry high-status advertising, they address a middle-class audience, they have high-quality photography and glossy paper.

16 Men.

17 It offers personal identity gratifications by addressing fandom, by featuring role models and by reinforcing values; it offers social

interaction and integration gratifications by showing companionship and content for real-life conversations; it offers entertainment through humour, eroticism, gossip, free gifts and striking visuals; it offers often detailed information on a wide range of issues, which gives a sense of surveillance.

Questions 4 and 5

1 Sans serif.
2 Modernity or informality.
3 Serif.
4 Tradition or formality or authority.
5 Multiculturalism, consumerism, celebrity culture, changing attitudes to gender and/or sexualities.
6 References to other media products that the audience are expected to recognise.
7 A media product that combines a number of different genres.

Paper 2 – Section B: News

Question 6

1 Guardian Media Group or the Scott Trust.
2 IPSO or IMPRESS.
3 Convergence.

Question 7

1 Tabloid.
2 Because of the idea of 'press freedom' – that governments in a democracy cannot interfere with the press.

3 Middle class (AB or ABC1), fairly balanced but slightly more male than female.
4 By appointing an editor with opinions similar to their own.

Questions 8 and 9

1 Sans serif before January 2018 or serif after January 2018.
2 Traditional mastheads in serif fonts, serif fonts for headlines, high ratio of copy to images and headlines, more formal language register, more restrained use of colour.
3 They use mostly serif fonts, whereas most websites use sans serif.
4 More closely cropped.
5 It contains much more soft news.
6 Democracy, human rights, individuality, diversity, tolerance, allowing opposing points of view, internationalism, seeking solutions to social problems, progress.
7 Fewer representations mean more stereotyping because under-represented groups often don't work in the media so nobody notices the misrepresentation.

Question 10

1 'Jackie: we're very happy' or 'Unions postpone strike'.
2 The article about a white man marrying a black woman or 'Briton shoots a gold'.
3 'So polite, the North Sea Spy Game' or 'Yard suspects Black used two-way radio' or 'America accused of spy frame-up'.
4 'Wilson–Brown market clash'.

Revision activity answers

Paper 1 – Section B: Promoting Media

Page 47

1 Warner Bros does not have to pay copyright fees for characters for which it already owns the copyright, so this saves it a considerable amount of money and increases its profits. The fact that the characters are already successful in previous films reduces the risk for Warner Bros in releasing a new film that is not part of an existing franchise.

2 Using successful characters in the promotion of the film would help Lego to sell merchandise, including toy sets and characters based on the film, increasing its profits and promoting the brand. The sale of Lego merchandise then serves to further promote the film and creates more income for Warner Bros. This means that both industries benefit from their relationship.

Page 48

1 It is important for regulation to exist as media products can be very influential on their audiences. If the film and video game industries were not regulated, there would be more chance of audiences accessing inappropriate content, which could have a detrimental effect on their development. Regulation also ensures that media producers create content that meets acceptable standards in terms of moral and ethical perspectives.

2 Some people suggest that strict regulation goes against media producers' right to freedom of expression – essentially, this means the freedom to create whatever they want without rules or regulations to abide by.

3 A 'censor' is an organisation that 'deletes' any content that is seen to be unacceptable. The BBFC clearly felt this term represented it in a very strict and overly authoritative sense, so changed it to 'Classification' instead.

4 In order to make profit at the box office, the right certificate is important. If an action film achieves a 'U' or 'PG' rating, it is unlikely to contain the levels of violence and danger that fans of the action genre would want to see. Similarly, if an animated film aimed at very young people achieves a '12A' rating, it may be excluding a large part of its target audience and therefore be unable to make the profit the producers would hope for.

Page 59

1 They were so keen to work with Lego because they knew the brand's popularity would help to sell their own products. Therefore, they decided to pay the production costs themselves to guarantee the deal.

2 One of the most appealing factors of *The Lego Movie* for audiences is the way the whole film is made of Lego – just like fans of the toy will immerse themselves in a 'world of bricks'. Therefore, the marketing team ensured each advert reflected this world entirely consisting of Lego, even down to the logos of each company being made from bricks.

3 Each time we see one of the main characters from the franchise, we are reminded about the film and therefore the main promotional message – that audiences are encouraged to go and watch the film and should be excited about seeing it.

4 The target audience of the film is a family audience – ranging from young children to the parents who will take them to the cinema or buy the associated products for them. Therefore, it is important to strike a humorous tone that will appeal to a wide range of people. The way in which the couple in the BT advert interact, for example, will appeal to more mature audiences whilst the appearance of the *Lego* characters and the world made of bricks will appeal more to the younger generation.

5 Vinny Jones and Lenny Henry are fairly well-known figures from the film and television industries. Therefore, fans of these celebrities may be encouraged to go and see the film once they have seen them promoting it. Furthermore, they may find pleasure in the humorous way their voices contribute to the animated versions of these well-known celebrities.

6 Six million people is a lot! It is especially impressive to reach that many people when you consider the number of TV channels available these days and the amount of choice audiences have of what they would like to watch on TV. It is great for both *The Lego Movie* and the featured

brands because they both gain a lot of exposure to potential audiences and therefore more people may go to see the film or use/support the featured brands.

7 It is important to remember here that not all media audiences respond to texts in the same way. Some audiences may have enjoyed the ad break, found pleasure in the humour and felt excited about the release of the film. However, some audiences might have seen the ad break as simply another way to encourage us to spend our money, and therefore felt 'turned off' by it. This may be especially true of older, more mature audiences who have been exposed to a huge number of adverts and forms of promotion over their lives.